About the Art of Being Alone

How to overcome loneliness and the fear of being alone while learning to love yourself

Copyright © 2017 Janett Menzel
13359 Berlin

Independently published.

ISBN: 1548945285
ISBN-13: 978-1548945282

This work and all its parts are protected by copyright. Any unauthorized utilization without consent from the author is prohibited. This particularly applies to its electronic or otherwise reproduction, translation, distribution, and provision to the public.

This too shall pass.

— SHAKESPEARE

CONTENTS

Preface	7
The Enemy in Your Head	18
Exercise: Me and my parts	23
Exercise: What others could share with me	24
Exercise: Decisions or what I did instead	27
Test: What type are you?	30
Do not fear yourself	57
The Nature of Things	61
Exercise: The poles and antipoles of my emotions	65
Inspiration and creativity	68
Why it is worth confronting anxiety	71
Finding Treasure in the Mud	79
Exercise: Looking for the hidden treasure	87
The Basics Against the Fear of Being Alone and Loneliness	91
Blame, Shame, and the Need to be Welcome	101
Beliefs and life patterns	102
Anger and Fear as Substitute Feelings	104
What Science Believes	105
What is Hidden Behind the Fear of Being Alone?	106
Loneliness in a Relationship	110
How Silence Makes Partners Lonely	110

Strategies to Experience Relationships Together Again	114
Strategies and Methods for the Advanced	120
Tip 1: The step-by-step method	120
Tip 2: Ways of compensating for inner footing	121
Tip 3: Your voice against fear and sorrow	127
Tip 4: Build closeness to yourself	133
Tip 5: What would you have to do for things to get worse?	149
Tip 6: Let your "real" feelings out	150
Tip 7: Look in the mirror and recognize yourself in it	151
Tip 8: Feel the pain that you want to process	152
Tip 9: Forgive your feelings	153
Tip 10: Fall in love again – this time with yourself	154
Tip 11: Recognize that you get what you want in order to learn something	155
Tip 12: Take your shadow and go	157
Tip 13: Autogenic training	159
Tip 14: Take the worst and make the best of it	163
What Loneliness and the Fear of Being Alone Taught Me	164
You Often Find the Greatest Lesson Through Emptiness	178
A Distraction Please! 54 Impulses for Activities	181

WHY ME – WHY US

Preface

"I care for myself. The more solitary, the more friendless, the more unsustained I am, the more I will respect myself."

- Charlotte Brontë, (Jane Eyre)

All of us are familiar with the stifling feeling of fear when we are alone or faced with a period of solitude. This feeling looms at Christmas, New Year's, on birthdays or holidays, while others are spending time with their families and partners, are surrounded by friends, or are feeling happy although they are alone. For lonely people, this feeling of fear and sadness can lead to so-called monophobia, the acute fear of being alone. But what do those who have learned to enjoy solitude do differently? Why are so many people able to enjoy the comfort of their relatives and loved ones, while others supposedly have to do without it? Is there something that we can learn from people who like to be alone? What can we do against the fear, loneliness, and the feeling of being lost and insignificant? How do we handle the desire for social contact, security, love, and friendship? Is it possible to overcome and unlearn one's loneliness?

My experiences have shown me that this is entirely possible. These days, I love being alone. I have overcome my fear of being alone. Today, I need time to myself as much as I need the air I breathe. But this was not always the case. When I was suffering from panic attacks and agoraphobia in 2013, things were quite the opposite. Without a partner and cut off from the world by fear, I had to learn once again that I was important, that I love myself, and what I could do on my own to feel good. I began searching methods and techniques. This book is based on all my experiences and features backstories, strategies, and opportunities for rethinking. Because what the fear of being alone represents and what causes loneliness is a wake-up call from your heart and soul. They want to show you what lies dormant and triggers all your emotions. They ask you to understand instead of just listen. They beg for attention and ask for reminders of your true nature. They do not know guilt or shame, only truth and profoundness.

From my work as a journalist and coach, there is one thing I know: most people are lonely but would never reveal this side of themselves publicly. They cover up their insecurity and loneliness and try to distract themselves, for example, through phone calls, social media such as Facebook, mobile games, or by making appointments. Even going out, to be surrounded by people, staying in contact, being seen — these feel like the only ways to get attention. Only so that they can meet with supposedly happy people and because they are afraid of being recognized in their loneliness and looked down on. Sitting alone at a table in a café or restaurant, eating alone, going to a bar, the cinema, or traveling alone — doing so alone makes them unhappy. You see how others are not alone, are laughing, talking, and have someone to share their experiences and feelings with and to talk to about them. Human contact is also about being needed, having a purpose, being important, and being thought about. However, constant feelings of loneliness can create the impression that no one is interested in you, misses you, or wants to know about you. It is a terrible feeling, causing emptiness, anger, isolation, shame, fear, and, above all, sadness. It can often become an illness, whether emotionally or physically.

While people like myself like to be alone, go for walks alone, enjoy peace, pursue their activities in a café, go out to eat on their own, or prefer to work for themselves rather than for a company, there is a great sadness raging within those who are afraid of being alone. It is not just because they are alone, but rather because they feel abandoned, outcast, or invisible. They feel like a small child who has lost their parents in a department store. They feel like it is their fault, that they are not worth much, or even both. They lose themselves all too easily in the belief that they have done something to cause their solitude.

It reminds me of my childhood. Before I was seventeen, I had lost all my attachment figures except my mother, whether through divorce, death, or family quarrels. My mother was "only" a nurse, which – like all social occupations – was at a financial disadvantage. Her divorce from my father and, above all, his living situation meant that he did not provide us with any support. My grandmother, who had held our family together, died. My uncle died two years later. My mother disassociated herself from my grandfather because of irreconcilable differences. She was alone with her young daughter, went to work in shifts, and, in between, tried to be a good mother. In doing so, she forgot to be human and worked her fingers to the bone the whole day. I remember that she used to sleep a lot. But she never cried, at least not when I was looking. She was lonely, but her survival instinct would not let her grieve for the events in her life, the death of her mother and brother, the loss of her father and husband, and all the cares that came with these. She kept everything inside. And in the meantime, there I was, six or seven years young, needing attention, and hungry for love and life. Instead, all I had left was myself.

I spent a lot of my childhood waiting. For my mother and her well-being, time that she owed me, for my father, for my grandpa, for answers and activity, attention, and security. But none of it was to be. In all my sorrow, my brain decided on the clever move of acquiring substitute feelings. Instead of sorrow, which would have completely overwhelmed me, I became angry and anxious. Today, I know that anger is a smokescreen for sadness. It is supposed to protect us, while preventing repressed sadness from resurfacing or even more disappointment from spreading. Fear is a very dear friend that fights a tough battle. It tries to create a balance between protection and activism. Although it shows you what is wrong and what needs to be worked on, in doing so, it conceals the true wounds. One by one, it allows the hurt from the past to gradually heal. It knows that everything has its time.

With years of loneliness, my anger also grew. If I read my journals today, I am deeply saddened: There are almost no entries that are just cheerful or that do not at least express any anger about the circumstances of my life. You would think I had been an aggressive child. But I never expressed my anger out loud. It just bubbled up quietly inside me. I directed my anger towards myself. In my fear, I tried everything I loved to hold on by hook and crook. I discovered reading and animals for myself. Books gave me the feeling that I was finding out something about the world outside and, at the same time, that I could learn something from it. Animals allowed me to learn unconditional love and loyalty as well as responsibility for my own actions and foreign life. If I had not had both things, I would be a different person today. However, through my anger, I unknowingly laid the foundation for my later anxiety and panic disorders.

Fortunately, anger and curiosity have a positive effect – they prevent moderate or severe depression as much as possible. Unfortunately, they do not protect from self-doubt.

And this is exactly what keeps us from believing in ourselves, standing by ourselves, and from seeing our goals through – come hell or high water – from separating ourselves from the bad, experiencing the depths of our feelings, and processing them. Doubts prevent us from making decisions, from having healthy self-esteem, and from wholeheartedly trusting that everything has a purpose.

It has taken me the past four years to understand this and to look into how our feelings and emotions work. Understanding is essential if we want to face ourselves. If you are now saying, *"But I don't want to face my buried experience at all!"* then I can well understand you. Fortunately, fear is a sign that you are ready and that your head is now able to do everything necessary to assess information and to put it into a new context so that you are better in the future. Without fear. Without loneliness. Without powerlessness, defenselessness, helplessness, sorrow, and anger over being alone. Nobody has to take these steps alone. If the feelings are too big a burden, professional help is always recommended. I myself sometimes discussed it in therapy, but I took the essential steps single-handedly. I did not feel at ease with the thought of somebody guiding me in finding myself. I wanted my pace, my way, my method, and my objective.

To do so, I first had to find out what had led to my feelings of loneliness.

When I had my first panic attack, I was alone. I had it as I was feeling left alone (professionally) and was reminded of the past: of my anger. A few years later, my agoraphobia spread. It was once again a time when I was on my own in professional life – partly voluntarily, partly under duress – and it would be there to stay. Interestingly, my body always reacted with fear and panic whenever I felt alone. There was nothing left for me to do except learn to be alone without feeling bad and to learn to enjoy my time to myself. What had made me so sad and angry that I became "ill"?

I had to question everything, separate myself (from the old), and learn unconditional self-love. In order to love yourself, you have to know or get to know yourself. People who are lonely usually do not know themselves or do not know how to appreciate their positive sides. Everything looks like a bottomless pit. You feel like you are entirely dependent on the sympathy and permission of others. It is not uncommon to get the idea that sticking by yourself easily comes with loss. However, for lonely people, more loss means having less footing and security. This makes you afraid.

Back then, I did not know where to begin. Should I look for new hobbies, a new partner, encourage more activity within my friendships, learn new anti-anxiety strategies, or quit my job? Instinctively, I decided that I wanted to keep my fear as a shield. I rejected all notions for psychiatric drugs and set out to find myself. I discovered how few passions I still had and which ones I hadn't acted on for years. I remembered everything and everyone that had unconsciously and unintentionally encouraged and demanded my self-alienation. I learned to look behind my own façade as well as that of others. I trained to be a writing therapist in order to expand my coaching expertise. I consumed every piece of literature on the subject of fear and the mind that I could find. I devoted myself to my dark sides (the mean or self-serving, unilateral, and partly hurtful intents of my ego). I cried a lot about everything I was missing. I let out my anger through sports, which I could "finish" in under 10 minutes at home. Agoraphobia and panic attacks come with the physical feeling that "outside" is like a war zone. Some people do not leave their house for years. But I forced myself because I had no other choice left. I had my anger. It allowed me to face my fear and people who are, well, not so much the pleasant type, but rather the people in whose company you can only keep calm if you have learned to be assertive or at least have inner peace. So, I learned both. I learned to accept help from people who knew better than I did. I learned to help others and, through my work, also to be able to be happy for others. I started to write again and got myself two female cats. I began to commit myself to other people and to use my abilities for the good of others. In short, I allowed myself to see my life differently, to fill it, and, in doing so, to fulfill it.

I learned exclusively through one motto that my therapist had once entrusted to me: *Do it for as long as you want it, until someone says STOP or until you have found a different solution.* Therefore, I learned to use my problem-solving capabilities and to live more according to the principle "Nothing ventured, nothing gained". I made mistakes on purpose, deciding in the morning after waking up, "Today, I will let myself make five mistakes and see exactly what happens." I learned that I did not have to be perfect and how to handle rejection and criticism. Above all, I learned that I was just as important as the rest of the world, that no one was "to blame" for my circumstances, and that no one could change the past.

I knew that if I did not start from scratch, my anxiety and anger would settle in my body and provoke even worse illness. We believe that we own our body and that we can direct our feelings for the most part. We are even more surprised when our body lets us know that it is an illusion and that it simply does what it wants at any time – even against our needs. It is exactly the basic feelings, such as disgust, shame, sadness, and fear, that often dominate us. We can however reduce them so that we are not unconsciously and helplessly at their mercy, but rather prepared and solution-oriented. We can accustom our mind to not experience certain situations negatively. Our brain allows it.

Behavior therapy shows us that short changes in our lives only work in the short term. However, those who want to experience an entire future full of satisfaction, whether alone or not, have to hold out. Balance and personal happiness are not a light switch. The light only comes on if many conditions within our responsibility are fulfilled and if there are lights that have the correct light bulbs, a paid electricity bill, etc. This is just a trivial example to invoke an even simpler one. At some point, everything is "empty", like the good wine that you drink or the jar of Nutella whenever you want to indulge yourself. We have to learn to stand up for the fullness that we want in order to have a fulfilled life. And for that, we have to know what and who we need to be happy.

Today, I know myself. I experience every day consciously and decide precisely how I want to spend it. I no longer do anything that is not good for me or makes me unhappy. I do not have to use every possible contact so that I am not alone. I love just as much to retreat to my world and recharge my batteries. I experience my social contacts (friends, family, professional network) as safe and loyal. Christmas, birthdays, and other "social and warm" times are made for me. I no longer wait for the annual holiday abroad in order to finally get "out" or let go. Since my fear and panic, I ensure that I am relaxed and learning new things, feel good, and have fun every day. I have had to make cancellations and separated myself from painful relationships and friendships. I have found my ways for the times that make life hard.

This book is aimed at helping all those who feel alone to find themselves again. I wish you every success in the process and, above all, a lot of resilience with the necessary longing to one day achieve what makes you feel alive. Be worth it.

All the best on your journey,
Janett Menzel

THE NATURE OF LONELINESS

The Enemy in Your Head

*"Our deepest fear is not that we are inadequate.
Our deepest fear is that we are powerful beyond measure.
It is our light, not our darkness that most frightens us."*

- Marianne Williamson (A Return to Love: Reflections on the Principles of "A Course in Miracles")

The fear of being alone and of loneliness, together with sadness, are extremely paralyzing feelings. We are ashamed of our neediness, do not want to bother the lives of our friends and families, or we have had experiences that make it difficult to trust people. For many who are alone, because their partner has died or they have separated from them, a sudden, unfamiliar emptiness is the order of the day. This can quickly turn into the thought of supposed uselessness and, not uncommonly, depressive moods. People without partners, whether wanted or unwanted, experience loneliness in a similarly desperate way. They all associate with a basic feeling, which is often called a "belief pattern" in psychology: *Something is wrong with me, because…*

- I am alone.
- I was abandoned.
- I do not have/cannot make any friends.
- I do not have any family.
- I do not have any hobbies or passions.
- I am different to other "normal" people, for example, not as social, not as happy, not as brave, etc.

This basic feeling shows three extremes. Firstly, as people, we like to be liked and, therefore, often orient ourselves around other people (and what they think about us). In order to not be alone, to be part of a community, and to be welcomed and valued, we are prepared to do quite a lot. Secondly, in doing so, we often forget our own direction in the flow of our lives. We hide our opinions from others or forget to have them. We adopt goals and values that have little or nothing to do with our own. Between these extremes, there is yet another component. Being alone, because you already recognized it. Just because you did not want to be like the others, you have distanced yourself so that you would not reveal yourself and driven yourself into a kind of social isolation. What was missing were similar people with similar interests and thoughts, as well as ways of distancing yourself while still being able to express yourself.

In my work, an extremely interesting fundamental conflict between these extremes quickly appeared. People who are alone and/or feel loneliness are more desperate for what others think about them or even their solitude than the circumstances that surround them. This is due to the effect described above. However, being alone is more difficult with all the associated feelings if we carelessly believe others' thoughts about us.

If there is no one who affects our emotional state with their beliefs, then we look for titles and solutions for the problem within ourselves. However, consulting the ego and letting it decide has not just been difficult since Sigmund Freud. It either blames us, because we seem to have done something wrong, or we are so convinced of ourselves and our thoughts that we do not dare to look at countless possibilities and solutions.

In order not to see ourselves as separated, we often make one mistake. We do everything to be included. Within this goal, there is, however, a crucial problem that pulls everything difficult in an even more negative direction. We believe that we have to be different in order to no longer be alone and to be wanted, needed, welcome, important, and valuable once again. We ourselves grasp at the slimmest straws. This only happens because we remember times when we could share and others could share with us. We miss fullness, comfort, warmth, security, and contact. There will always be times when one or all of these needs goes unfulfilled. What can we do then?

What would happen if we remembered ourselves – in our true nature? I ask this question because the fundamental "problem" of being alone is not being alone itself, but rather the desire to take part. We give up something to reach this goal: US. We forget who we are, were, and wanted to be in favor of companionship. This is why people remain in bad jobs, one-sided or hurtful relationships and accept great pains and illness in order to be able to still be of use for others. Because they dread being alone and the feelings that come with it and because they have forgotten that every person contributes to the bigger picture and forms a part of the community. We decide what we do and do not give. The links in the chain consist of individual people who willingly share what they have plenty of with each other. Particularly, people who experience being alone because of separation or loss feel that way because they feel *separated*. They were used to sharing and being shared with. If one of these parts breaks away, then something is missing. This is because the formerly supposed whole smashes into its individual pieces. Suddenly, you see yourself again and do not always like what you see.

In order to keep this book as effective as possible, I would ask that you view the good and the bad as a whole and, at the same time, perceive yourself and the others as separate from one another. This perspective will help you to see *yourself in your true nature* and still get in touch with what you desire from and with other people. To support you in this, you will find a small exercise on the next page that should help to unravel the entangled thoughts.

Exercise: Me and my parts

Grab a pen and find your answers to the following questions:

What do you have to give?

What do you have in abundance?

What are your strengths?

When do you feel lovely?

What were you always able to do better than others?

Which of these would you like to share?

Exercise: What others could share with me

What do you admire and envy in others?

Why is it that others have/can do these things?

Since when have you noticed this?

What have you done to change this?

What do you believe you must do but shy away from doing?

Why are you afraid of it (e.g., an experience)?

What are you shutting it out for?

What could happen if you dared to do it (even with your future fear)?

What would have to happen for you to feel secure?

When do you feel loved?

Do these moments match the answers to the question, "When do you feel loving?"

For many of my readers, obstacles arise at this point. One of the most common obstacles is the following, in various versions:

- *I am not concerned with giving. I would like to receive.*
- *I have given for years. I am like an empty vessel. I need content.*
- *An experience made me feel like something was taken from me. I believe the world owes it to me to make up for this imbalance.*

A second is this thought: *I no longer believe that I have anything to give. My loneliness gives me the feeling that I am not worth anything (to others), good for nothing (for others), and cannot do anything (in others' eyes).*

From the self-reflection questions, you will have noticed one thing: It is our thoughts about something that control our feelings. If we, therefore, work on our thoughts, we also change our feelings. If we manage to think fewer negative thoughts, then we have succeeded in having fewer negative feelings. And it goes a step further still. If we succeed in thinking positively instead of negatively, then we have also succeeded in feeling good instead of bad. Despite being alone. In doing so, we escape victimization, helplessness, and uselessness. By reminding ourselves who we are and reaching a decision to change a situation. Hence, in the following is another exercise that should help with this.

The difficulty of decisions is this: The word "decide" literally means "to cut off" in its Latin origins. When we decide something for us, we automatically make a cut with a person or something (e.g., a job, a hobby). In doing so, we reject it. The more conscientious we are, the more difficult it is for us to come to a decision for ourselves and against someone else. Those who often base their decisions around others will struggle more with loneliness and fear than with being alone itself. Hence this reflection exercise. Listen intuitively to your gut feeling when answering the questions.

Exercise: Decisions or what I did instead

Which big decision that you were proud of can you still remember today?

Which big decision that you regret can you still remember today?

What made you regret it? Was it people or was it a feeling?

If it was a feeling: Where did it come from? Did it come from you?

Were you "given" and "talked into" it?

What big decision did you want to make but avoided out of the fear of rejecting or being rejected?

What did you do instead of this big decision? What other steps did you always want to take in your life without doing it?

What did you do instead?

For the benefit of whom or what did you do it?

What other steps did you always want to take in life without doing it?

What did you do instead?

What other steps did you always want to take in life without doing it?

What did you do instead?

In order to be able to make decisions, you have to know where you are coming from (start), where it should lead (goal), and how to get there (way). Therefore, I have developed a test that should show you what your type of solitude is.

Test: What type are you?

For each question, answer with the number of points that apply most to you. 1 represents a little, while 6 stands for very frequently. If you wish to give a question 0 points, leave it out. The question then counts without points. Please answer the questions spontaneously.

Do you get anxious when you think of being alone or are faced with a period of being alone?	1	2	3	4	5	6
Do you notice especially on holidays, birthdays, and celebrations that you are alone?	1	2	3	4	5	6
Are you missing something in your life that nurtures you, even when everything goes haywire?	1	2	3	4	5	6
Do you have palpitations, weak knees, a lump in your throat, great inner restlessness, and the urge for immediate action whenever you are alone?	1	2	3	4	5	6
Can you name at least five aspects of your life that you are thankful for?	1	2	3	4	5	6
Are you able to trust the people in your life unconditionally and always, with all their weaknesses?	1	2	3	4	5	6
Do you reach immediately for the phone or do you have to obsessively get out when you are alone?	1	2	3	4	5	6

Do you feel well and in good hands in the world?	1	2	3	4	5	6
Do you have passions and hobbies that you love and carry out?	1	2	3	4	5	6
Do you have difficulty and unease thinking about and deciding what you want to do when you are alone?	1	2	3	4	5	6
Do you spend fewer than seven hours a week with yourself and your hobbies (also evenings together with close friends)?	1	2	3	4	5	6
Do you feel guilty whenever you are alone?	1	2	3	4	5	6
Do you bypass times of solitude with food, drinking, work, sports, or sex?	1	2	3	4	5	6
When you think of the future, do you feel little to no confidence and self-realization?	1	2	3	4	5	6
Do you often think of past times when you enjoyed more social contacts and hours in others' company?	1	2	3	4	5	6
Do you feel senseless and useless whenever you are alone, as if you are not able or allowed to do anything like a child?	1	2	3	4	5	6
Do you miss somebody or something in your life so much that it sometimes takes your breath away?	1	2	3	4	5	6

Do you feel like you have little to no independence and freedom in your life?	1	2	3	4	5	6
Do you find it difficult to get into the activities you love and lose track of time?	1	2	3	4	5	6
Do you have the feeling that you have to function rather than be allowed to live?	1	2	3	4	5	6
Do you feel incomplete and imperfect on your own?	1	2	3	4	5	6
Do you often feel sad whenever you are alone?	1	2	3	4	5	6
Do you feel like you have to wait for your life or love (also without understanding)?	1	2	3	4	5	6
Do you feel like you are not good enough for your dreams and goals?	1	2	3	4	5	6
Do you often long for social, strong, and caring contact?	1	2	3	4	5	6
Do you feel unease at the words *self-efficacy* and *freedom*?	1	2	3	4	5	6
Do you believe that being alone is a punishment for you?	1	2	3	4	5	6
Do you react sensitively to criticism, rejection, and impossible demands from others?	1	2	3	4	5	6
Do you often like to withdraw when everything is too much for you?	1	2	3	4	5	6
Do you have difficulty sleeping and/or staying asleep?	1	2	3	4	5	6

Are you a perfectionist and only feel good if you have achieved something big?	1	2	3	4	5	6
Do you long to know someone or a group of people with whom you can share your interests, problems, and thoughts?	1	2	3	4	5	6
Do you believe that there is no love and closeness for you?	1	2	3	4	5	6
Do you wish for others to profit from your strengths?	1	2	3	4	5	6
Are you unsatisfied with the way your life is now?	1	2	3	4	5	6
Do you have depressive moods such as tiredness, states of exhaustion, brooding, and desperate moments with deep sorrow and/or fear?	1	2	3	4	5	6
Would you only need one or two new hobbies or passions to find yourself again?	1	2	3	4	5	6
Do you believe you need to be in a relationship to be happy?	1	2	3	4	5	6
Do you feel useless when you are not needed?	1	2	3	4	5	6
Are you very concerned about others' opinions of you before and after conflicts?	1	2	3	4	5	6
Are you familiar with the desire for extreme closeness and then extreme distance?	1	2	3	4	5	6
Are you mistrustful of new people and situations?	1	2	3	4	5	6

Your total points:

On the next pages, you will find your result. Should your point total verge on another result, it will show your tendencies and possibilities.

Results and classification

0-24 points

It looks as if everything is wonderful for you. Congratulations!

25-50 points: Disoriented boredom

You feel bored. Do you feel like you lack direction, ideas, impulses, and goals? Ask yourself:

- What/who brings me joy?
- What can I immerse myself in completely and forget time?
- What passions and hobbies did I have in the past?
- What was I good at in the past?
- What have I always wanted to learn?

Draw new impulses for your lifestyle from your answers. Bring more action into your life by discovering yourself in your needs. The world has numerous opportunities to offer you.

Your boredom may be accompanied by fear of (even more or lasting) emptiness. If you manage to focus on your positive growth, this anxiety will disappear. Until then, you can distract yourself from your anxiety using relaxation techniques, friends, family, enjoyable activities, and purposeful leisure time. Sports and other physical activities help you to break down your stress hormones and to direct your attention towards worthwhile activities:

- Which activities make sense for you and which are pointless and difficult?
- Which activities make you feel fulfilled?
- What does an activity need to have to be worth doing?

51-100 points: Diffuse anxiety

Your number of points indicates that you anxiously experience boredom when alone. This anxiety can surface before being alone, throughout, and during solitude. It is very likely triggered by a depressing experience of emptiness. People who often had to wait or did not learn how to be alone and were often interrupted in their solo activities report having this diffuse anxiety:
- Are you somebody who often spent your life waiting or spent a lot of time alone in the distant past?
- Are you a person that has always avoided having empty periods of time without activity and/or people?
- Were you rarely left alone in your life?

- Were you often there for others or was your free time filled up with meaningless activities? Did you always have to do something?

Suddenly being left to yourself, on your own, feeling helpless and useless, paralyzing feelings, because you do not have anyone to share their time with you. All can be reactions that lead to your anxiety. In such moments, remind yourself that you are an adult today and capable of functioning. You decide what you do, for how long, and if you do it.

Fear is easier to grasp when you determine its source. Ask yourself the following questions:

- Why am I afraid of being alone? (Which experience in the past reminds me of this?)
- What is the purpose of my fear of being alone? (What benefit is it to me if I am afraid? What does my fear allow me (to not have to do)?
- What did I do in the past against this fear?

In these situations, it helps to do something with somebody as a friend and helper. This can be someone from your circle of friends or acquaintances or a therapist, coach, psychologist, etc. Together, you can establish a plan of how you can deal with this feeling the next time. The chapter "Strategies and Methods for the Advanced" describes the first tip of this "step-by-step method" in more detail.

But you can also meet this challenge alone. Breathing techniques, relaxation techniques (especially progressive muscle relaxation and autogenic training), and contact with nature (going for a walk with your cares and fears) achieve very good results with diffuse anxiety. Also, cultural, manual, creative, and sensuous experiences, such as art, music, good food, films, literature, painting, photography, gardening, handicrafts, sewing, etc., relieve the left, rational side of the brain that is responsible for broodings and fears. In oppressive situations, you can directly do something for the right side of your brain in order to stop interpreting and emerging fears. Above all, occupy yourself with *meaningful* and *enjoyable* activities. Find something you could love. It will nurture you in times of diffuse worries and fears. You will notice that your brain will quickly adapt to the change of direction.

100-150 points: Sad loneliness

This number of points suggests that you feel lonely and sad. Loneliness may be accompanied by depressive moods, states of exhaustion, and anxiety (attacks). Experiences of loss, the feeling of not being wanted, and, primarily, helplessness thereby play just as large a role as uselessness and the feeling of not being needed. For this reason, the loneliness may also feel as if you were left alone or even abandoned. You lack moments in which you feel valuable and appreciated. You place times alone on the same level as times where you were (supposedly) left behind and unloved. In doing so, feelings of fear, sadness, and brooding become dominant – caused by wounds of the past. Ask yourself which situations in your life have made you feel exactly this way:

- Were there similar moments in your childhood where you were without your parents or other attachment figures?
- Were you allowed to learn or even experience joy on your own through the experimental games of a child?
- Were your activities steered by your attachment figure?
- Were you allowed to learn to participate (willingly) naturally?
- Was the nature of attention and care forced on you?
- Were you allowed to learn to express your needs?
- Did you have a relationship that made you feel cramped or brought you more distance than you wanted?
- Did you unconsciously adapt to this partner (out of the fear of losing them)?
- Did you have a job (or do you have a job) that does not allow individual strengths but is rather only intent on functioning?
- In which areas of life are you able/allowed to run free and which not?

I have deliberately used "able/allowed to", because many people who are confronted with fear and loneliness live excessively through external control. Their life feeds on what they receive from their surroundings. They define themselves through it. What others judge as their value, becomes their identity. They give themselves little to nothing.

Find yourself again. Become the person you want to be. Rediscover yourself in your needs and allow yourself to set goals that you pursue *for* and *because of you* instead of for and because of others. The following questions may help you to get to know yourself again:

- What/who brings me joy?
- What can I completely immerse myself in and lose track of time with?
- What passions and hobbies did I have in the past?
- What was I good at in the past?
- What have I always wanted to learn?
- Which activities make sense for you and which are pointless and difficult?
- Which activities make you feel fulfilled?
- What does an activity have to have to be valuable?

In order to delve further into your type, I will describe the four forms in more depth in the following. The fourth form, anxiety, I have deliberately split up. It is not only involved in all types but also appears as an originator or reaction.

The Four Types of Being Alone

Strictly speaking, there are no types of being alone, as it is about our thoughts and the feelings that arise from these in combination with circumstances rather than being alone per se. One such circumstance is emptiness. Loneliness is an interpreted form of being alone while being alone is only a circumstance, a form of emptiness. It also appears in couples and all kinds of relationships, even when other people are present (or, in theory, take part in our life). Merely the interpretations that emptiness brings with it can make certain times difficult. For some people, being alone or feeling emptiness may only mean boredom but not loneliness. In turn, others react with fear and loneliness when alone. Find out what it means for you using the following classifications.

Type 1: Disoriented boredom as the cause

People who are bored have either nothing to do or the activities that are on offer are meaningless. Again, there are feelings associated with this. You lack enthusiasm, have difficulty concentrating, begin an activity that you quickly finish again, feel inner unrest, or are irritated or listless, because something is not successful or does not bring you joy (anyway). You sleep more than is necessary or are so much inside your head that your body begins to rebel. The emptiness on the inside tries to fulfill itself through external actions. This also includes distractions such as watching television or eating. You have increased hunger and cravings for sweet or savory things. If you then lack ideas or social contacts, an even greater emptiness arises, which can siphon into sadness and negative thoughts.

Boredom can also cause fear. The fear of relaxing, doing nothing for a moment, and setting everything down is mixed with the thought "No, but I have to do something!" It also shows a fear you may have, mainly of occupying yourself while alone or looking for something that is truly fulfilling. No later was the term burn-out coined than its opposite, bore-out, appeared. It denotes a painful underload in working life, which in turn can trigger depressive moods and burn-out.

An underload is also difficult in private life. Having no task or meaning is especially miserable for people who are looking for self-esteem, respect, and self-expression. Those who want to give something to the world, participate, and contribute something or are social will suffer more from boredom than others.

- Are the usual ways perhaps too retracted or the daily tasks too meaningless?
- Do you only spend your free time with the same people and need a social change, new intake for your head, or people with similar challenges and interests?
- Or do you have absolutely no time for yourself where you can busy yourself with subjects that are important to you?

In order to regain your strength, it is recommended that you find new hobbies and passions or resurrect old ones. What did you enjoy doing in the past? What have you always wanted to learn or do? What do you do instead?

This brings us to a further aspect of boredom: overload. Boredom often surfaces in people who overload themselves or have been overloaded with duties and responsibilities. They then wear one out so much that boredom arises in order to force us to relax. Here, it is worth finding out what makes us so demotivated and listless.

- Which areas wear you out?
- What about a certain activity makes you feel troublesome and strained?
- What would have to go away so that things feel light again?

Specifically searching for the causes helps to brighten up your mood again, because you are spending your precious time on something that is *really* important to you. Enjoyable things are everything that makes you happy and allow you to express yourself. Close your eyes and allow yourself to be led by your inner voice. Which impulses come to the surface? What do you really want to do? What is your body signaling to you that it needs? Then open your eyes again and start doing it.

Type 2: Emptiness as the cause

Whenever we are alone, we sometimes perceive ourselves and our life as empty, unfulfilled and meaningless, disoriented, and, in good time, even futile. Some typical thoughts are, "What am I supposed to do alone then?", "How am I supposed to go off on my own?", "What am I supposed to do outside, where everyone can see that I am alone and have nobody?" Many people need a reason, a person, or external justification to feel secure, welcome, associated, and held. Especially when they are in public around people. If, on the other hand, they only want to go for a walk or shopping alone, it means less to them that they are without company. It is, therefore, the social moments that they experience alone that prey on Type 2 people. The possible thoughts of other people increase the pressure for self-justification. For a long time now, being alone has no longer been something well-received. In the past, managing on your own was a sign of survival power, independence, and strength.

Nowadays, however, emptiness is mistaken for missing something, meaninglessness, or futility. Emptiness actually only means the absence of fullness, not abundance. In turn, being alone means "being" and "alone". You still are (no more and no less), even when you are alone. Being alone is therefore less about a feeling than the *circumstances*. At the moment of solitude, you are the only one who counts. But you are not empty. You are not nothing. You have time for and with yourself that you can spend however you choose. You do not need to pretend or achieve something. You decide for yourself how you spend the time. There is not much more to say on the matter.

The difficult thing about being alone is however the fear that it will remain and that the state could continue far beyond your own limits. Here, emptiness is misinterpreted and mistaken with *trained importance* by other thoughts, for example with belief patterns:

- If I do not do anything, I do not achieve anything.
- If I do not achieve anything, I am nothing.
- If I am alone, it is definitely for a (negative) reason.
- If it is for a reason, this means that I have done something wrong.
- If I have done something wrong, I am not enough.
- If I was enough, I would not be alone.
- etc.

These belief patterns have been set in us since the days of our childhood. Back then, we saw the world through the dependent eyes of a child looking for security and, from it, learned what there was for us as a child to learn. But this pattern remains with us into old age if we do not accept that, as adults, we do not have to do anything that we deemed important as a child. Today, everything is different. You do not have to do anything at all. What was useful then may be counterproductive today. Even that what you believe or learned to be "true".

Being able to occupy yourself with fulfilling activities when you are alone is beneficial for the mind and soul. It gives you the feeling that you have a meaning and a purpose even though you are alone. People who feel bored when they are alone are often looking for that ONE job, that ONE sense, that ONE partner, or that ONE hobby. The world has a lot to offer. Find at least two things in your life that nurture you and give you a comfortable feeling whenever you are alone. These should be activities that you can fall into, grasp you, and sweep you away in order to divert your attention from everyday life.

Activities that specifically bring *joy* are especially ideal. But social involvement, insofar as it does not drain too much of your strength, can also give a bored person more meaning and fulfillment again. You can achieve this especially well with creativity and intuition: painting, photography, writing, crafting, needlework, handicrafts, building... The number of possibilities is sheer endless. The main thing is that the right side of the brain strongly relieves the left, abiding by the motto: When the hands are busy, the mind is silent. Whichever passion you choose, these should be activities that allow you to express yourself – with everything that you are and feel. This keeps the psyche healthy and brings balance into your life.

Type 3: Loneliness as the cause

Being lonely means that you feel separated, as if you do not belong, cut off, excluded, invisible, unimportant, and forgotten. The feeling of loneliness is the discrepancy *between the real and the desired* relationships and social contacts in life. Therefore, the feeling of being lonely is a subjective assessment that does not have its authority in real life. Above all, loneliness means the feeling of isolation, painfully experienced boredom, and pain due to human reactions such as envy, jealousy, and sadness about what others have that they are missing (or that they feel is withheld from them).

With this type, there are two extremes:

"Waiting people"

Waiting people adapt themselves to take part. To do so, they put up with a lot. For example, being part of it but not being allowed to take part. They may certainly give but rarely take. It is a high price to pay. As such, they gradually fall into a waiting pattern. They wait for their partner to come home, someone to call, their friends to get in touch, to be wanted by someone, to become important, to achieve something great, and to get something specific for it. It is only then that they believe they are valuable. It is not until they have achieved something with or through others that they have "earned" their worth. This is naturally a fallacy.

You are already worthy. Perhaps you don't believe me. This script pattern, as transactional analysis calls it, is so deeply embedded in your system that no other truth can reach you. This is why it is immensely important that "waiting people" recognize their chances to control their life even if it scares them. Many people have not learned that they are able to discover and guide themselves (because they themselves have given the permission to do so!). They take small rejections as a rejection of their individuality, as if they were not allowed to become "great" or orientate their own life as they want like an adult. They have only gotten to know their own paths and steps, ideas, and talents with resistance. They have learned that peculiarities and obstinacy either hurt and scare off other people or lead to conflicts and their own fears of loss. As children, important attachment figures perhaps said to us:

- Don't make Mommy/Daddy sad!
- Be a good boy/girl!
- Don't always be so rebellious!
- Mommy really loves you but not when you are being like this!

As children, we constantly try to find out which qualities and behavior promise us maximum security and footing. If our parents suggest that we should be quiet and nice, we will also display fewer conflict situations and less disruptive behavior later in life. Security through (forced) harmony becomes an exchange deal that damages us later. In this way, we do not learn that we have a right to our own opinion, are allowed to say no, express and demand our needs, desire reciprocity, and bring further development and individuality to our life. The result is that people who experience loneliness and fear perceive "being how they are" almost as a danger. They often adapt their emotions, such as anger, feeling alive or loved, to the environment or conceal them.

However, authenticity is the first step towards living. Even when our world today enjoys following the silent admittance that there are rules to be kept, it is normal to question your learned rules in times of loneliness and fear. Letting feelings be, allowing yourself to feel anger and rage, disappointment and fear, and perceiving helpful and healing impulses from the situation is the first step. Acting according to them is the second. Even if we have not learned to act independently and stubbornly in our childhood, it does not mean that we are not able to catch up on this at any time. We only require life conditions and social contacts that fit our true identity. It is not our environment that decides what nurtures us, but rather we who decide whether the environment is good for us. The more discrepancies there are, the more difficult it is to endure lonely and frightening feelings. The antipoles are missing: joy, sense, security, love, a sense of belonging, independence. As life is not always easy, more and more situations would automatically come along and demand new adjustments – and the loss of yourself, your identity, your desires and dreams, needs and goals, and your values. In such moments, a shift would once again take place. You would once again forget that your boss, circle of friends, family, partner, children, colleagues, acquaintances, etc. are only human, just like you. On the same level, with the same level of importance, and the same value. Just like you, they have the right to authenticity.

Despite this, the rules of cooperation apply to them: Respect towards others, perceiving and preserving others' limits, listening, and much more. However, they will only do this when they see that you have limits that you perceive and protect, defend if necessary, and sustain in conflicts, while you remain respectful, listen to the others, and still stick to yourself. Leaving yourself out of fear, being left, or hurting someone is not an option if you want to banish loneliness and fear from your life. Therefore, we have to first behave if we want to get what we want. If we desire more authentic and nurturing contacts in our life, we deliberately have to find out what nourishes us and then look for like-minded people. We have to be authentic again instead of adapted in order to avoid emptiness and have something/somebody to fill. We have to find out what holds us back from having contact, a relationship, a fulfilling job, or something similar.

And with that, we are at the second extreme:

Anger and sadness lead to isolation

An equally large group of people who suffer loneliness combined with fear and sadness block access to others. They withdraw themselves because they were greatly hurt inside by situations where they were rejected. I am deliberately speaking in the present tense, because they are still this way – whether the wound was inflicted far back in the past or first began to bleed last week. It remains open and can be torn open again by the painful experience easily and at any time. Understandably, this group is afraid of getting hurt again.

What does our head do in moments such as these? It confronts us either with deep sorrow, which makes us feel worthless and unworthy of love, or it reacts with anger and fury so it does not have to admit the sadness. Before a situation can become painful again, the fear or anger is already there to prevent the sadness coming into our lives in the first place. We play through scenarios in our head, how we would react to them, and lift ourselves into a state which in turn allows (and requires) us to retreat. We self-justify ourselves.

In this case, it may be that the depths of the sorrow are too difficult to bear so your brain protects you from them. Extreme anger would then trigger rather fear and panic, quickly skipping to a different form of pain and sorrow, but leaving the actual wound untouched. In this way, our spirit allows us to gradually approach what it needs to be healed at our own pace. Confessing that we are hurt in this moment, because… or if a situation reminds us of an experience from the past, is very helpful. It takes the energy from the force of your angry and annoyed feelings.

In these moments, you should ask yourself what you need to stop feeling this anger and fear. Usually, impulses such as "Tell them what I think!", "Ask again what they meant!", or "Forgive!" appear. Following these impulses is a better idea than aggravating them.

Reentering the conversation is also easier than forgiveness. But in actual fact, all people are different and getting close to them with new trust will be easier than persisting in despair over failed encounters. We do not know what tomorrow holds or how situations are going to change. There is no 100% truth. Every person has their own views. However, many have not developed any feelings of compensation or do not want to feel them.

Just like depressive moods are always a call to face and recognize the darkness, we are now prompted to find a light within us that we can follow for a better life. This requires consistency and support. When the depressive moods have changed into depression worthy of treatment, this primarily means that you should look for professional help and a trusted person who you can share your feelings with. It is also advisable to look for like-minded people, for example, in self-help groups (online or nearby) or people who have gone through the same. There are some subjects that you cannot face alone. You don't need to either. For some subjects, you also need a protected space to be able to face them.

Of course, there are mixed forms. You can well recognize your current mood from your own body language. People who frequently stand with legs that are crossed or pressed together or cross their legs when sitting stifle what is inside them. People who, in turn, keep their heads down or their shoulders tense are more prone to sadness. People who prefer to sit or stand outside in public, near doors, or at the edge of groups of people tend more towards the second extreme.

It is similar with people who indicate the complete opposite. They want to be right in the middle, always need someone around them, constantly want to be in a conversation and occupied. They are usually very empathetic and sensitive in order to perceive the needs of others and adapt to them. But if these reaction areas are missing, they lapse into a sadness (loneliness) that feels as if the rug has been pulled from beneath their feet. They feel lonely even in relationships and during group activities because they are unable to express themselves in this environment as they are used to. Consciously changing your posture in such moments helps the body to allow a mental change.

This is because loneliness also suggests that it is a lasting condition. In times of loneliness, we often forget that we can act or even how many contacts we have and that the world is open to us. It scares us to feel lonely, because we feel abandoned and helpless. Overcoming loneliness is therefore about stepping out of the passive state into an active one.

This is why, in coaching, you turn belief systems around: from "I was abandoned" to "I abandoned myself" and from "Nobody is helping me" to "I am not helping myself" or "I am not looking for somebody to help me." In active language, these sentences sound very accusatory, but they reveal a truth that cannot be denied. They have their sense. For example, it would make sense if you did not look for anyone that could help you. It could be because you would rather overcome it alone or because you are afraid of looking weak with your feelings. Just try to remember:

- When and why did you start to become removed from yourself?
- Who gave you the feeling that weakness is "weak", "troubling", "problematic", and "improper"?
- Who gave you the feeling that nobody could help you and that you had to manage on your own?

Please do not regard these as shameful or guilty, but rather as an invitation and indication that you can and are allowed to become active. You decide how and what with, how fast and when, with whom, and how far.

Form 4: Paralyzing fear as a <u>foundation</u>

Fear is a primary or primal emotion. We were born with it. Fear has its justification and sense as well as disgust, anger, sadness, joy, and (depending on the scientist) some others. It benefits us by making us act in times of danger in order to ensure our survival. However, fear can also be a symptom and disguise. It then behaves exactly like anger as a disguise for sadness. Or it goes hand in hand with sadness.

In order to reduce fear, it is best when we look behind its two-fold nature. Ask yourself the following questions whenever you feel fear:

- Why are you afraid? (past experiences)
- What are you afraid for? (What does your fear allow you (not) to do? What does it want to protect you from?)
- What would have to happen for you to take your fears into your own hands and still take action, even if those fears would rather grant you protection?
- Which fear is greater – that something bad will happen if you ignore your fear or that you will remain lonely if you act despite of your fear?

Make yourself aware, in a loving manner, that we only have to do what we want to have to do. One saying goes: *No one has to suffer. We ourselves decide for whom or what we willingly suffer.* People (who have become) trained to function and fit in normally find that difficult to believe. Due to earlier or new experiences, the fear stirs within us that we commit mistakes and could suffer from them (or be hurt by others' mistakes). That's why we prefer to remain in old, wasting situations that damage us rather than pursue new paths. We fear rejection, failure, and criticism just like we avoid pain. It is because of fear that we abandon activities where we could fail. Initially, we do not accept any contact with someone out of the fear of being rejected. We do not challenge ourselves because we have already previously had degrading experiences, for example, where we failed. We do not meet the new challenges of unfamiliar situations because we have no assurance that everything will go well and that no danger is lurking. We take old situations with the feelings of that time and place them over the current one. We imagine that we know all people and are able to assess the future using our past. Our brain has taken notice of it and obediently stored it. If a situation then enters our life that makes a reorientation necessary, this first runs neuronally through our decision-making center. That is where we determine whether we leave it (because we believe we know how it ends anyway) or whether we try again (and deliberately counteract the old fear).

THE FOUNDATIONS OF FEAR

Do not fear yourself

"There are two basic motivating forces: fear and love. When we are afraid, we pull back from life. When we are in love, we open to all that life has to offer with passion, excitement, and acceptance. We need to learn to love ourselves first, in all our glory and our imperfections. If we cannot love ourselves, we cannot fully open to our ability to love others or our potential to create. Evolution and all hopes for a better world rest in the fearlessness and open-hearted vision of people who embrace life."

- John Lennon

Where fear comes from is only then important when we look at it and consciously want to work on it. From my experience, most people orient themselves towards the potential danger through rejection. This is not only about other people. We ourselves have needs that we cannot fulfill. We want to be perfect or implement everything immediately and effortlessly, without resistance or obstacles. If it doesn't happen the way we have envisaged it, then we are annoyed and frustrated. We throw the activity back into the corner, just like children who still struggle with resilience and patience.

But fear also plays a large role when we do something for or because of other people. This is because there is a resonating feeling that it has to be perfect or come with the promise of special love. If we do not receive the attention or care, or only moderately, we then land back in the trap of displeasure. In moments like this, we lack a clear decision and strategy for our own life.

People who seem to manage everything effortlessly and almost never fail have one thing in common, they do not give up until they have achieved what they wanted to achieve. They overcome hurdles, critics, and kilometers just to reach their goal. Inside, they have the certainty that that is the goal they want to pursue. The cause of this is not important. The price is normally the same. It is called rejection. Not only do they have to reject others and ignore all resistance from some people, but they even have to step on a few toes and accept that they have distance themselves because their goals do not match ours (any longer).

What certainty also implies is that you trust yourself and, therefore, are trusting. You believe in yourself and your goal. You trust in it because you know what you can do and that it will succeed. For this, you have to be responsible for your goal, just like product brands do with their consumers. If they didn't think their product was good, did not advertise it or offer it anywhere so that we would not see it the supermarket, they would be gone from the market in no time. And nobody would ever benefit from their product. I don't want to compare anyone with food or consumer products. My point is that the backgrounds are the same. If you do not know your strengths and values, goals and paths, you get stuck in your situation and only a few people will ever learn that you are there and how much you have to give and to share. This is also a fear, but it is one that you can control. For this reason, ask yourself the following questions:

Which fear is greater

Is it the fear that you will remain alone because nobody finds you? Or *Is it the fear that some people will not want you, while others adore you?*

For 95 percent of all people, the first question is crucial. It shows that they are entirely ready to advertise themselves. They know their worth. But the fear of rejection resonates nevertheless, even when it is less decisive than with the second question. The second question is more attractive for people who are willing to accept everything and everyone without seeing who and what is actually suitable (and who and what is not). These people quickly suffer the consequences of bad decisions, which sets the vicious circle of being alone, boredom, loneliness, and fear back into motion.

However, both groups have a hard time becoming a "problem", being uncomfortable, or disruptive. One thing is certain, we will not be able to convince everybody. Think of your favorite chocolate or favorite fragrance. Some people like it, just like you. And others would rather buy a different product or different variety.

While we are sure that a decision would be the best **for us**, we know (or learn over time) that it was problematic for others, caused trouble, or involved a lack of understanding. We do not care about this in regard to unimportant matters because we hardly create meaning for us as a person. People are however more sensitive to connections and relationships. While some have learned that it is okay to have a different opinion and there is no threat of loss just because there are differences in opinions or debates, others are afraid of conflict. They have learned that they are punished for having their own paths, goals, values, and opinions – with distance, less love and attention, imposed work, or being alone. They became more careful, tried to compensate, or avoided similar conflict situations. The more unwavering the other person remains, the more insecure we became. Separation or marginalization are a further consequence that can settle down as a feeling. It felt as if we were punished because we apparently did something wrong, were "bad", or not enough. It was just one thing: a difference in opinion and not enough steadfastness. However, everyone who feels solitude, loneliness, and fear as a burden needs exactly that: assertiveness, consistency, obstinacy, and self-confidence.

People who know the feeling of being a problem well also shy away from triggering it in others. We don't want to be hurt or hurt anyone else. We don't want to be perpetrators or victims. How it led to solitude and where the loneliness came from is no longer important. We mix everything together and make a soup out of it. If the inner emptiness, the longing for love and to be needed, participation and belonging, the urge for security and warmth spreads, then we remain stuck in the feeling. We then do not make any decisions with and for ourselves but are rather distracted (by others) or again persist in brooding and defending ourselves internally.

However, the solution would be to work with ourselves by coming to a decision for us. However, our mind is unfortunately trimmed to find "the guilty person", even in us, if necessary.

The Nature of Things

All of us try to avoid and repel fear.[1] Whenever we are afraid, it is mostly about threatening losses and failings if the thing or person is very dear to us and/or plays a large

---

[1] Some people rejoice in the so-called "Angstlust" (lust for fear). They feel the ultimate kick through the adrenaline secreted and, correspondingly, enjoy exposing themselves to frightening situations. They deliberately evade psychological fear defense mechanisms.

role in our well-being. Worries about the future often arise, how it would look if…, what would change if…, and what we would lose. Everything that appears valuable to us now threatens to leave or is already gone. This fear of loss goes hand in hand with separation, a feared surgical cut that we are not ready for, for which we believe we have no answer. In this victim's role, we lose touch with ourselves. Our identity is lost and the thought that we are immobile and can only look on helplessly triggers anxiety.

Therefore, during our life, we develop many strategies to dodge such fears. These are called the natural defense mechanisms against anxiety. According to the renowned psychoanalyst Verena Kast, overcoming the fear starts immediately when the fear sets in. I would first like to explain the most important coping mechanisms in order to demonstrate afterward how these mechanisms can also help you.

Distancing

When we pull ourselves out of the fear using distance, we then say sentences to ourselves such as, "Calm down! Relax! Take a deep breath! Relax and think!" This relaxes the body and is effective against the physical fear response. Through this decrease in symptoms, we are in a position to distance ourselves from the frightening situation. We view the thing from a different perspective, with distance.

Rationalizing

We often associate distancing with rationalizing. You don't need to be afraid, you shouldn't be afraid, calm down and don't suddenly lose it.

Rationalizing also means analyzing a frightening situation to death. It is about no longer wanting to feel the fear.

If, through our many worries, we ourselves take the opportunity to do something about our fear, we usually "fetch" somebody else, whether just for advice or for a responsibility that we cannot currently bear. This person then becomes the savior in the emergency, who "takes" our fear from us in the truest sense of the word.

Projection

When a fear is not tangible and we are unable to say exactly what is causing it, we often unconsciously turn to projection and project our fear onto someone or something. With relationship fears, we usually hear ourselves say that he/she does not love us anyway. In professional life, we focus on colleagues who "bully" us and only want bad things for us. Private financial problems are projected onto our landlord or someone else. Therefore, on the one hand, you have a reason for the fear to exist. On the other hand, we make our fear artificial and easier to handle. If we can give the fear a name, we can cope with it more easily.

According to Kast, the difficulty is looking at yourself and sticking by your fears instead of directing all the weight towards one person or situation. The true fear comes from within.

Validation

Whenever a potential degradation scares us or we fear that we will experience loss, we validate the situation or rather the person themselves. In extreme cases, this leads to contempt. We then say that this person had always been strange, the potential employer would have paid badly anyway, or the coveted partner was not attractive enough anyway and we deserved something better. We lead ourselves to believe that we can "wing it" in order to be able to grasp and endure the triggers of anxiety.

These natural defense mechanisms are used in all situations and dimensions of emptiness. One of the most effective strategies against fear, misinterpreted solitude, boredom, and even loneliness is therefore the rethinking of automatic thoughts.

According to Kast, what is important when reversing the fear is that hope, inspiration, and joy are seen as the antipoles of fear. The following exercise should help to provide you with more information about these poles.

Exercise: The poles and antipoles of my emotions

Which feeling is the worst when you are alone?

Which situation still triggers the worst feeling?

Which feeling is the opposite of this feeling?

Which situation/action triggers this feeling?

What makes you happy?

Which situation would give you hope?

Who do you know that is familiar with these feelings?

How you can use your answers

Which feeling is the worst when you are alone? You should therefore work on this feeling in the background and not on the means of compensation or escape. However, we do not make it worse than it is by bringing it up, but rather simply call it a project, for example "Project Fear". The feeling is then put into the center, and we are willing to try everything to relieve the feeling like with pain. We do not stop until we have reached this goal.

Which situation still triggers the worst feeling? If you can name other situations in which you have this feeling, and also if it is less intense, you can first use these to transform the feeling. This makes the first step easier and gives your brain the chance to get used to the new behavioral method. Just like a football player has to pass through several test matches and training sessions before he goes to the stadium on an important match day, you can test and examine yourself.

Which feeling is the opposite of this feeling? It would be ideal if you succeeded in generating the opposite of the negative feeling a bit like antidepressants do. Then we would do something that makes us happy and gives us hope when we are afraid and panicking. Or we would switch to courage and optimism instead of being sad and hopeless.

Which situation triggers this feeling? One idea is to try to achieve exactly these opposite feelings through targeted actions that lead to the feeling. It always made me happy to paint and write when I was scared of having panic attacks. So, I painted and I wrote – for hours if I needed to. Indeed, I noticed latently that the actual feeling was still there, but I had taken over control of this impulse myself. This gave me strength and allowed me to cope with the panic.

What makes you happy? Every person should be able to name at least three to five activities or things in their life that make them happy. In this way, you can maintain resilience in difficult times. The more often we do something that makes us happy, the lighter our hearts will feel. The less often we are happy in our lives, the harder it is.

Which situation would give you hope? Classically, it would say here that there are situations where you no longer feel lonely, but rather secure, welcome, and useful, because you are valuable to the world, your town, your community, your municipality, your colleagues, your family, your relationship, etc. This is therefore your goal.

Who do you know that is familiar with these feelings? It is helpful to exchange with somebody who has gone through or is going through the same. Together, you are strong when you work on one and the same feeling at the same time and learn from one another. Find somebody, ideally from the same city.

Inspiration and creativity

According to Kast, an entire field of emotions go hand in hand with anxiety and consists of tension, fear, panic, anguish, grief, rage, aggression, and anger. The latter two, in particular, go hand in hand with a common anxiety defense mechanism: attacking through aggression and anger. But if this is directed towards oneself – that is, if the anger and aggression are only in our head and do not come to the place they should/belong – the negative spiral restarts. The significance stays buried, and we are not able to develop ourselves any further.

The German author Almut Schmale-Riedel explains the term *physique* in her book "Der unbewusste Lebensplan" (The Unconscious Life Plan). This term was originally coined by the developer of the transactional analysis, Eric Berne. In 1970, he wrote that there is a power in people that drives them to advance themselves, "to make progress and learn from mistakes"[2]. This power strives for further development and is a creative power of nature. Berne considered it a source of energy, which sent people impulses that motivated them to grow. It stands for change. Schmale-Riedel says that this power strives for perfect health and progress because it develops from the physique. Other people would call the so-called physique the soul.

No matter whether you grew up in a destructive family, live in a one-sided and unsatisfying relationship

---

[2] p. 86

today, are unsatisfied with your working life, or still only function on the surface: The soul or physique motivates people to constantly strive for autonomy, self-realization, self-enablement, and self-empowerment. In her 1992 publication "Transactional Analysis Psychotherapy", Patricia Clarkson wrote that this physique strives "for the greatest possible fulfillment of the good"[3].

According to Schmale-Riesel, the physique/soul is about interpretation and seeking meaning. It prevents the worst life circumstances and external influences from leading to the loss of obstinacy. Self-enablement, the energy for growth, longing, and freedom, always survives because of our soul.

No matter how lonely you feel, if you manage to perceive the physique or soul, you can empower yourself to use the energizing, inner core to heal yourself.

Countless scientists have confirmed in publications that creativity is a channel that allows the physique or the soul to express itself. This may also be the reason that methods of art therapy or writing therapy work quickly, far-reaching, and with lasting effects on people with psychological troubles. Creativity makes it possible to break blockades and creates a way of unloading submerged feelings and hidden emotions. Those who believe in the principle that negative energies (negative thoughts and experiences) build up and remain stored in the body and cause stress, fears, and sadness in the long term can profit very much from creativity.

---

[3] p. 29

There are countless ways to be creative. Some people enjoy painting. Others prefer writing. However, needlework, crafting, baking or cooking, web design, illustration, drawing comics, kneading clay, pottery-making, screwing, repairing, decorating, etc. are also creative activities, as are gardening, collecting, and even cleaning. Creativity is about moving from the left, rational side of the brain to the right, emotional half. The more we bustle in the left side of our brain, the more we brood and let ourselves be controlled by interpretations of our ego. If we do create something, then we create a new circumstance through ourselves.

Anybody can creatively heal fears, depressive moods, panic, and every form of stress by finding a creative channel that matches their personality. In this way, they can deal with symptoms because they allow them to be released from the head, body, and soul the moment they appear until far back in the past.

The fear of being alone or any feeling that is experienced while being alone strongly resembles the symptoms of "normal" anxiety, stress, and depression:

- Typical anxiety conditions are trembling, shortness of breath, palpitations, weak knees, a lump in the throat, insomnia, inner restlessness, feeling trapped in oneself, stomach, bowel problems, concentration problems, panic attacks, vulnerability to infections and colds, fear of

unconsciousness or dying, circulatory problems, and many more.
- Radicals! Self-responsibility is difficult.
- Deep-rooted fears and aggressions that erupt into silent anger or tantrums, auto-aggressions, and nervous breakdowns.
- It activates and reinforces belief patterns, which lead to broodings and thought clouds of doubts, blame, and shame, resulting in a partially extreme exhaustion.

These doctrines are, for example, *I am not allowed to be here. I am guilty. I am not alright. Love is dangerous. There is no love. The world is evil. Something bad will happen if I am alone.*

Thinking and checking these doctrines during a creative activity is a bit like going for a walk with your worries. Whenever we are in motion and whenever the right side of our brain is activated, it is easier to overcome any kind of worry, fear, and grief. I invite those who cannot free themselves from their broodings to select a creative activity of their choice and to reconsider everything burdensome during this activity. You will notice that the worries do not feel as bad – and disappear through the channel.

Why it is worth confronting anxiety

It seems appropriate to me to light up the other side with positive aspects. The perspective of those who have no trouble with being alone, those who do not feel loneliness, those who can provide some information. How do they look at the state of being alone? How do they experience solitude? How do they spend their time? What does it mean to them and what meaning do they see in "lonely" times?

1) New fuel for your reserves

When your car runs out of gas, you don't just leave it where it is, never drive it again, or curse and hope that it refills itself. Spending alone time with yourself can be like gas for an empty car tank – away from people, away from outside influences, away from the unfamiliar. It allows you to return to yourself, to see your inner self, and to spend time with yourself without unfamiliar demands and external qualities, or needs or conversations. These are all stimulations and influence the body, which in turn needs strategies to process them. Time alone can be like meditation. In this time, you can process everything that has happened to you and, also, what remains. You reorganize your feelings and objectives and reflect on yourself and others. All of this is necessary to maintain the view of the valuable things in your life. During such times, you can distance yourself if others are too present or too much in the center or if your interests and opinions fade into the background.

2) The ability to be alone improves relationships

Most people suffer from being single because they have difficulty enduring times alone or do not know how to fill them. What's more, they would love to have company so that they could share their life. Sometimes we confuse one for the other and it turns out that we are only longing for *someone* because we do not want to occupy ourselves with us. This is completely natural in my eyes. Humans are not made to be alone. They need community and integration. We are made just for herds and packs.

However, a downside of being together may be that we would rather (like to) occupy ourselves with the concerns of other people than our own. This does not make our life easier; it is in no way better led. But those who can be alone can enjoy time with others more. Those who feel lonely when alone are normally only satisfied in relationships, where there is company around the clock, because they are actually empty inside. How much nicer would it be if we would look at our sides that we do not live and love, work on them, and develop what we hope to find in relationships and friendships?

Our relationship with ourselves is the only important one in life. If something is not right with this or if it is dependent on external expectations or conditions, other relationships (in our career, circle of friends and acquaintances, family) may not be authentic and nurturing. In extreme cases, we are or become dependent or we act as the footing for others that we are so desperately searching for ourselves.

3) Rediscover and reexperience independence

Being independent also means that you are not attached to anything or anyone. You are relaxed and free and can go wherever the wind takes you. You can do and leave what you want – run around like a slob with greasy hair and undone fingernails, party with your friends into the night, lie around on the sofa in a onesie and with chips, drive out into the countryside instead of working through the household chores, watch the ducks, or shop for hours, surf the internet, read a great book, or stay somewhere as long as you want, and indulge in our hobbies however we like. There is no one to interrupt you with warnings or worries, to demand, or to place their views higher than yours.

Vice versa, there is also no one that you have to worry about. You are solely responsible for yourself. You decide what you do and if you do it. You decide if you let it be. This is what people who enjoy solitude love most about it.

Moreover, many people who do not want a relationship specify this point as one main reason.

4) It strengthens your self-awareness and self-confidence.

The more time you spend with yourself, the better you get to know yourself. It may sound crazy, but getting to know yourself also means being able to assess whether you like spending time with yourself or not. If your answer to that is NO: You have no other choice but to make what you want to out of yourself. Which quality do you find less great to have? What would you rather have? More peace, more activity, more motion, more nature? Create a list of the more unpleasant qualities and then an extra list with the ideal ones that you see in others and would like to fulfill in yourself.

Start very small. A few steps today and another two, three steps next week. Take the time you need to get to know and love yourself. This develops strength and faith but, above all, confidence for the times that are more difficult. Become aware of who you are (alone) and who you (alone) need.

With this question, many realize that they do need solitude in some moments. It is only the other hours, which are felt as lonely, that are depressing. This can be due to all kinds of hidden reasons: hobbies that are dependent on external factors (sports classes at specific hours in specific places, passions that are cost-intensive, etc.), too few contacts with close friends, too little willingness to travel or discover, not having a group of people with whom you can share your values and passions, rather adapting yourself to the passions of other people/friends in order to not be alone (foreign hobbies or meeting points), looking for places where people are instead of where you are alone (to prevent comparisons in the first place), not suggesting anything "new" to your friends/acquaintances, a low willingness to learn (for new hobbies, further development of abilities, and qualifications), or suppressed desires for a partner (out of fear or still unprocessed grief about a painful loss).

This point is also about a formative belief system, which "assesses" the feeling of loneliness and makes a judgment. This sounds like, "I need other people to be happy and content" or a variation of "I can't do anything alone." But in truth, you would also meet and get to know people in activities alone. Not all of them may become potential friends or acquaintances straight away, but the greater the number of people, the more likely it is that a handful of people can be found with whom you can and would like to establish a close group.

From my experiences, I know that people tend to either be very selective or not selective enough. This can make it more difficult to get to know new people. But with some practice and confidence, you can take a closer look and recognize who does and does not fit to your personality.

5) Leave time and experience time

It sounds crazy, but being alone is one of the most effective relaxation techniques when stressed and overwhelmed. Being allowed to experience time is one of the basic spiritual needs of a person. It is not a coincidence that so many people today become sick from stress and rushing around.

This "hurry, hurry" principle sets the body in a state of constant alertness, causes stress hormones, especially cortisol and noradrenaline levels, to rise, and triggers long-term mental problems and physical illnesses. Setting all tasks aside for a moment, leaving the place untidy, leaving the dirty dishes until the weekend, and using the time for yourself instead of squeezing in an appointment in order to take a deep breath, take a nap, or lie in the bathtub. Consciously doing nothing is difficult, but it can be learned.

The positive effects are countless. Give yourself a break and enjoy your time in your own way with yourself and for you. Even a few minutes are enough to separate yourself and be alone. Integrating these minutes into your routine every day will protect you from the next cold, evening insomnia, or the constant inner unrest.

During lonely hours, this is easier said than done. Therefore, start with short sequences. Take two minutes or 10 as your goal, instead of expecting several hours from yourself. During this time, try to perceive yourself consciously and meditatively, without evaluations. Stride through the world as if you are an observer on a mission. Look more closely at the buildings that you know whenever you go past them. Look at the people more consciously, especially the positive *and negative* sides. In the morning on public transport, it is easy to see how stressed, annoyed, and moody some people are. You can see who is a morning person and who isn't. Simply observing means perceiving – without judgments or interpretations about yourself or the supposed "ideal" world of the other person.

This is what people who can be alone and enjoy it do. They perceive the people around them, but they neither judge their position in the world nor interpret their own through the eyes of other people. They are simply there. They also know that everybody has problems – with themselves and their life. No life on this earth is free from doubts, trouble, anger, fear, sorrow, etc. There are merely people who are better at hiding it. Whenever you are in the town and see people laughing and not being alone, but rather spending a nice time with friends or their partner, it does not mean that everything is love, peace, and harmony for them. They may have problems in their career, with money, with their child, or with an ex-partner. They could have health issues or be stuck at an impasse. One thing is certain, everyone has their own problems.

RESILIENCE: THE ART OF DEFYING
ADVERSITY

Finding Treasure in the Mud

"You can either be a victim of the world or an adventurer in search of treasure. It all depends on how you view your life."

- Paulo Coelho (Eleven Minutes)

Negative experiences weaken us and often drain us of important energy for enduring life's heavy blows and confronting them with assertiveness. Psychology calls the ability to still be able to do so resilience. This refers to the psychological power of resistance of falling back on sources of strength during times of crisis. This could be family, a relationship, friends and acquaintances, job and career, children, passions and life goals, hobbies, nature, animals, commitments, and much more.

Unfortunately, these resources thin out during life on their own or age-related factors and health restrictions make them painful to impossible. Isolated living locations, children moving out, death, the loss of a partner and individual family members, or a lower level of social contact with previously close friends are just some life events that can hinder lasting resistance. However, aside from external circumstances, there is yet another blockade that can make an intact resilience fragile: us ourselves.

We often forget that strength does not mean that you do not have any negative feelings or even weaknesses. Strength means a lot more, that we persevere despite difficult circumstances, mistakes, the unexpected, and burdens of life. We defy a breakdown by refreshing ourselves with the important aspects of our lives and summoning up new strength there. If we lack soul food, such as social support on individual or all levels, life's storms can be more than just laborious. However, it helps to become aware of how much strength you really have – in comparison to the little strength that we consider real:

- "I was hurt too badly!"
- "My last relationship broke me! I can't go through that again!"
- "My experiences have taught me that you can't trust anyone!"
- "My life has shown me that it is better for me to be alone!"

And other persuaded lack of strengths does not only weaken our actual energy but rather lets us believe that it is true. And yet, it is only a story that we tell ourselves to protect against fresh pain.

But how weak are you really? Or to put it differently, *How much strength would you have to save yourself if there was nothing left for you to do but to act for yourself?* Depending on which question you ask, the answer often changes. "Very weak" then becomes "a lot of strength".

I consider the crux to be today's society together with the media, the dominating online communication and altered structures of society, that make us people believe we do not have all the same chances and risks and are dependent on success, work, wealth, a relationship, family, etc. The internet is full of millions of articles that spell out for us everything we have to do before we have even gotten out of bed in the morning: Seven things you have to do to be healthy, five truths you should live by if you want to be happy, nine phrases you should never say to your partner, and 15 reasons to quit your job. In actual fact, we no longer even know what we are allowed to do. Eating cheese can activate cancer cells, meat eaters die earlier, and large cities are not only lonelier but also more mentally unstable because people no longer have any contact with nature.

The entire society is afraid of doing something wrong or being damaged or put at a long-term disadvantage through one misdeed. I would even go so far as to say that our society is afraid of death: from separations, losses, physical death, emotional death, and spiritual death. We are talked into believing that imperfection, obstinacy, authenticity, and individuality are mistakes and will be punished. Except if you are part of an accepted (because it has been scientifically proven), inherited, different grouping such as highly sensitive, highly gifted, empathetic, or handicapped people. Those who are completely "normal" and want to stay that way are faced with the problem of either offending through their imperfect personality or having to hide their true face. This includes their own needs that want to be fulfilled and which trigger longing and sadness when left unfulfilled.

Those who are said to be "too needy" and too unadjusted are looked down on and, in the most extreme case, excluded. We have removed ourselves too far from making our individual decisions, taking our life as it comes and mastering it, because there is nothing else left for us to do and we want to live. We latently or consciously follow others' rules and suppress our true nature from the first day of our life, adapting ourselves, and obediently joining in the game of the current society and culture. If it had not been for some people, for example, I would never have written this book. Why did I still do it? Because I trusted myself, knew my strengths, wanted it at all costs, and am part of a group who is accepted – the creative people who do their thing anyway. And although they may somehow be strange, they sometimes create something valuable. You understand what I want to say.

But here is the good news: Some few, completely "normal" people, and there are increasingly more of them, have managed, despite and because of their individuality, to use their obstinacy for what psychology calls resilience. They don't care about what someone writes or says about what people have to do nowadays. They simply do only what they want to do and believe every day that it is the right thing for them. If they notice that it is an obstacle, then they let it be and do something different. Naturally, they also have to learn how to deal with any criticism, rejection, worries, and doubts that arise, like those that have been accepted. They also have to learn to control their fear of failure. Because it is not only creative people who are deeply affected when their work is criticized or even torn up. If you look at the many shit storms on Facebook, you know what the people who no longer want to adapt at all have to put up with. "But how can you risk it?", "Everything that you're doing is pure idiocy!" are the fundamental notes of these hate speeches, when those conformists want to explain to the "disobedient" that they are behaving wrongly and are also wrong. And despite everything that faces them and their work, they simply carry on.

What distinguishes these people from others? Actually, just one thing. They look after what gives them inner footing more than what other people want to dictate to them. They are able to distance themselves. They nurture their indestructible beliefs. They doubt the dictations right from the first awkward intonation and recognize:

This is someone who shuns change and differentness, growth, and progress. This is someone who would rather submit to their fear than defy it. It is less their own fear but rather that what others have.

Only this one form of fear, that is, the fear of one's own greatness, is evident. Therefore, they prefer to stay small and feel insignificant back in the mud of the conformist masses than stand out because they are as they are. They do not know their caverns or their open waters – they deny their weaknesses and chances and worship their supposed strengths so strongly that they cannot break anything as long as they remain within the predetermined limits of society. If somebody else, however, has a special strength and power that they both know and show, it is immediately said by many sides that they are full of themselves and consider themselves better or more special. Believing in yourself and your uniqueness is a massive endeavor today if you have great things planned. For example, *becoming yourself* and daring to live that way.

This is therefore where resilience comes into play. Crucial factors like support from groups such as family, belonging to a community, and values that promote team spirit, which resilience research called "shared values", are not always present. Even if, according to theory, people who have these factors are classified as especially resilient, this does not mean that people who lack something in this area are automatically unable to be resilient. This is because resilience has no specific size. You can promote resilience by consciously and actively working on the obstacles. Being able to calm yourself, recognize avoidance behavior, and express your feelings instead of suppressing them can lead to a greater resilience exactly like another crucial ability – asking other people for support and advice.

If, in such moments, we still only hoped for social support and would remain at a standstill without it, so many great developments in the history of the world would never have existed: cars, electricity, telephone, the internet, as well as equality and democracy.

When we have no one behind us and no one to hold our hand, there is nothing less for us to do but to become this person ourselves. It helps to possess the following qualities and abilities:

- Expectation of self-efficacy
- Stubbornness
- Persistence
- Willpower
- Visions
- Imagination
- Mental strength
- Emotional resilience
- Communication skills
- Problem-solving skills
- Self-belief
- Knowledge of our strength

Other crucial factors that can support resilience include realism, beliefs (religiosity), being able to perceive senses, intelligence, impulse control, low fear of the future, the active shaping of relationships, confidence, value orientation, determination, acceptance, tolerance, conscientiousness, and the assumption of responsibility, as well as adaptability. The good thing is that all of these abilities can be learned. Those who have still not developed one or several points can therefore catch up on it and close their gaps on their own.

In order to find out which skill has still not matured and in which area most fears and great sadness occur, I have created another exercise. You will find several thought-provoking impulses for each skill. If you sense increased resistance with one area, this shows you that there is something important to learn and discover here. As usual, do not see it as a mistake or fault but rather as a welcome invitation to grow and develop into the person that you would like to be.

Exercise: Looking for the hidden treasure

Stubbornness and values
Are there things in your life that you absolutely persist in doing and which no one can challenge you on? Do you have limits that are impossible and for whose protection you would be prepared to do something? Are there things or areas of your life in which you quickly struggle when other opinions are expressed? Are you often quick to question yourself or an area of life?

Determination and responsibility
Do you have ambitions? Do you make plans, to-do lists, and checklists that you constantly work through? Do you often shy away from changes that affect your comfort zones or fears? Do you think about your fears and obstacles on the way to your goal, only to then decide that you won't pursue it? Do you have the courage to guide people and keep an overview of them? Do you shun responsibility when something is at stake? Can you put up with the weaknesses of other people? Do you put up with the neediness of people? Do you hide your needs?

Willpower and persistence
Do you easily abort activities when they don't bring you success straight away? Has anyone ever talked you out of ideas and opinions because they considered them harmful or foolish or believed that you couldn't do it? Do you prefer to work in a team? What do you trust yourself to

do alone? Are knowledge and learning an end in themselves for growth or a means to an end?

Visions and imagination
Do you have dreams that you have fulfilled? Do you actively have dreams that you would still like to fulfill? Are there societal, cultural, or social visions within you that are looking for expression? Can you picture in your mind how your dreams and visions would look when put into action?

Adaptability and impulse control
Do you react with pain, anger, fear, and rejection when somebody with a different opinion confronts, criticizes, or rejects you? Can you hold back, even when nothing is in favor of this? Are you able to accept that some things will never change? Do you actively work on things in your life that you can change? Do you quickly give people what they ask of you, even if there is little in it for you? Can you trust in the good?

Mental strength and intelligence
Do you regularly improve yourself? Is there somebody that you admire for their knowledge and journey? Can you stick to yourself even when someone vehemently challenges you? Can you distinguish foreign values, goals, and needs from your own? Do you have passions, hobbies, or a career in which you can topically immerse yourself in order to find new and interesting things about

it again and again? Do you read a lot? Do you prefer profound conversations or shallow small talk?

Emotional resilience, confidence, freedom from fear
Do you quickly give people what they ask of you? Do you often get annoyed at people or yourself later and wish you had reacted differently? Are you often embarrassed about your words and actions? Do you feel at fault when someone does not find you very likable? Do you carry on difficult conversations or conversations with difficult people in your head although they have ended? Do rejection or potential painful consequences greatly scare you?

Communication skills and actively shaping relationships
Can you express your feelings, even negative ones, in front of close friends, family, or other attachment figures? Are you able to ask for advice and support? Are you able to listen without interrupting after a certain amount of time and directing the conversation towards yourself? Can you give other people space as well as intimacy when they ask for it? Can you calmly carry out discussions with a respectful tone of voice when it comes to your needs and possible disappointments? Can you make concessions, even if they do not completely coincide with your attitude? In relationships, do you play the active part or more passive part who wants to be guided and led?

Problem-solving skills

Do you warn people about potential dangers or do you discuss possible solutions with them? In difficult moments of your life, do you look for solutions? Do you actively search until you have found a solution or do you give up in the middle? Do you view problems as challenges or as possible destruction?

Acceptance and tolerance

Do you find it easy to accept and tolerate people and concepts that do not fit in with your worldview? Do you frequently argue with people about their attitudes? Do you believe in your fears or even impose your paths and im/possibilities onto other people?

Self-belief and knowledge of your strength

Do you believe that you are secure? Do you believe that you can do everything? Do you know your rough edges and how you should deal with them? Are you able to use your strengths to improve your potential for development? Is it difficult for you to talk openly and honestly about supposedly difficult characteristics?

THE BUILDING BLOCKS OF YOUR
FOUNDATIONS

The Basics Against the Fear of Being Alone and Loneliness

"Guard well your thoughts when alone."

- Roy T. Bennett

It is worth delving a little deeper into the subject matter in order to gradually approach the entire theme of loneliness and what comes with it. Thus, I have gathered some facts that may provide some meaningful insights on the issue.

Firstly, those who feel most lonely are not older people but rather people under 30. When you are middle-aged, the feeling of loneliness decreases. It is not until well above 80 that the loneliness experienced reaches the same peak. This was discovered in a study by Maike

Luhmann from the University of Cologne and Louise C. Hawkley from the University of Chicago.[4]

Secondly, over 60 percent of all US citizens who feel lonely and alone are married or living in a stable, long-term relationship.

Thirdly, loneliness distorts our sense of reality. Because we feel emotionally lonely and separated, our mind tends to devalue our relationships, which (apparently) are not nurturing us, even more. All this is an attempt to repel our fear. It only takes one particularly intense experience of loneliness to forget the positive aspects.[5]

Fourthly, loneliness is infectious and transports those affected (as well as their friends and loved ones, who notice this loneliness) to a proverbial seclusion – mostly in the depths of social networks. This means that people are able to notice the loneliness, as far as you show your suffering. They then feel similarly lonely and also withdraw themselves (from other contacts). Those who hide their loneliness may appear strong and less affected by this scientifically proven mechanism. We, therefore, sympathize with people and the feeling of loneliness.[6] It is therefore advisable to confide in somebody who knows how to grasp this feeling and treat it neutrally.

Fifthly, loneliness causes the physical skin temperature to fall. You freeze. Participants of a study perceived

---

[4] cf. Luhmann & Hawkley 2016
[5] cf. Winch 2014
[6] cf. Winch 2014

a significant drop in room temperature just from remembering a lonely time.[7]

Sixthly, loneliness increases blood pressure and causes cholesterol to be secreted. This comes quickly in stressful situations, which is why our body also experiences lonely times as stressful and reacts in a similar way. It damages our circulatory and immune systems, making us more susceptible to illness. Any kind of social contact, therefore, makes us healthier and less susceptible to colds, flu, etc. At least in the long term. This is because short-term stress, when handled appropriately, is also healthy and partly even better than social contact. This means that we are healthier when we learn to direct short-term stress from loneliness and being alone in the right way; in which we act immediately in order to overcome the stress of the situation.[8]

Recall a stressful moment, where you were happy that you would soon be alone again. Perhaps it was a stressful day at work or you felt trapped and/or overwhelmed because of other circumstances, you simply wanted to go home, away from a group, away from other people – and be alone. Even the memory of this can retrieve feelings that your brain will reflect. Remembering moments like these calms you down when you are gripped by anxiety.

---

[7] cf. Winch 2014
[8] cf. Winch 2014

Accept that there are good and bad moments. There are, as you have seen, times when you are glad to be alone. In turn, there are also times when you feel alone and lonely. Such is life. Just like a sine wave in math class, it goes up and down, sometimes better, sometimes worse. But everything passes and nothing lasts forever. Even anxious or lonely moments will disappear again. As the saying goes, this too shall pass (Shakespeare).

I have repeated this saying like a mantra, like an affirmation again and again. It is like a formula that the brain has to learn. As if you were at school again and had to prepare for a test, you learn this phrase and recite it with constant repetitions. This does not solve everything, but it provides a short relief when fear comes.

Avoid social media at all costs when you do not feel good or feel lonely. As humans, we tend to compare and, at the same time, always put ourselves in the best light. Therefore, observing on Facebook how and that you friends are (apparently) doing better or what they are currently doing (whereas you are alone), draws a comparison with yourself in which you perform badly. It will only put you down and make you feel depressed.

The truth is also that happiness is always just a snapshot. However, seeing that other people are happy in this moment, while you feel less so will make you think that happiness and satisfaction are a permanent state for other people. It is important to look behind the façade and recognize that this is a misconception.

When anxious or lonely, avoid getting involved with the wrong people or those who make your connection one-sided or abusive, just to be with someone. Do not put up with one-sided relationships. Loving yourself means that you are allowed to be good to yourself and also that you recognize who is not good for you in order to avoid contact with such people in the future. If you were not, the person would be in the center, while you and your well-being would only stand in the way.

Help one another. Only dealing with yourself and poring over your own problems without receiving feedback is permanently bad for the soul. Being able to do something with others and "work" together on the challenges of life, having discussions in order to ask for advice, gives you the feeling that you are not alone. But it is important that you do not look for or hold on to contact for other reasons but rather directly address what is in your heart. That is how nurturing and mutual relationships are: open, honest, and beneficial. Beneficial does not mean always looking at life from cloud nine and pure sunshine. The right people know this and will see worries and/or fears as completely natural.

Look for people that you have something in common with, for example, a passion, a hobby, a sport, an opinion, an educational goal (professional development), etc. Being surrounded by people who tick similarly to you gives you the feeling that you are okay, instead of persisting in the thoughts that something is wrong with you and that that is why you are alone or lonely.

Avoid alcohol and other narcotics. The more you go into a stupor, the more terrifying waking up will be. Anyone who has ever tried to use alcohol to distract themselves from the burden of life knows that sitting alone with a glass of wine in your apartment will only trigger deeper sadness. The next morning, too, fewer things will be as nice as they could have been. This is because narcotics, above all, alcohol, are known for triggering intense fear, depressive moods, and panic attacks.

"When your hands are busy, your mind is silent." This is a well-known proverb. Occupy yourself with something that requires concentration, where you can let off steam and be creative. This could be anything from tidying to knitting or painting. How does this work? Those who are creative or physically active are not only in motion but also in the so-called FLOW mode. This is a state where you let yourself fall into and become absorbed in something completely. Some people experience this in writing or painting, speaking or drama, a particular sport, or with friends.

Whatever this one activity is – find it or revive it if you have neglected it in your life. I have known many people who had a passion but brutally neglected it, for example, singing or music, an instrument, decorating, being together with a certain group of people (e.g., children), or dedicating themselves to others. This point refers to a task that requires and fulfills you. Above all, it also means that you are needed and that you are fulfilled. Having a purpose, be it through an activity or a special feature, allows you to participate and feel part of something. Loneliness cannot arise here as it is based on being separated or feeling separated. Here, the world speaks of calling. The FLOW experience, which provokes deep feelings of happiness, is related to the professional environment, where there is not only a job or a career but a calling, an activity that comes to you. A sense that you provide when you live and give life to it. For me, it is writing. What is it or what could it be for you? Which passions have always made you feel fulfilled, excited, or happy (especially in childhood)? Sometimes, you have to dig a little deeper, as many passions were thrown away or abandoned because of criticism or lack of success.

The story that you tell yourself is not true. The pain, the loneliness, and your suffocating feelings will only increase if you tell yourself a story to help bear the reality. Stories like these consist of patterns and many untrue, destructive belief systems. They feed on victims and perpetrators, unhappiness and powerlessness, helplessness, shame, and neediness, which are felt as a burden (either for yourself or you believe that others see it as so). If the story has a happy ending, like in a film with a happy ending, then it makes you feel happy and stronger, even if the main character still has to have negative experiences and lessons. If it does not have a happy ending, then it is more similar to a drama or a horror film.

In stories that are told, there is always a hero that was awkward or self-destructive through negative characteristics or fears. It is more commonly wounds from past relationships or broken connections that are not patched up or able to be patched up (due to irreversible losses). Often at the beginning, the characters are still stubborn, anxious, or not ready to open themselves up emotionally or to reach out to someone. However, during the story, the hero or heroine is asked to reflect and change themselves through the experiences and to take their fate into their own hands and guide themselves to the future that they want. Through small steps and successes, you learn to see and appreciate the positive and to believe in the bigger picture. You have to find your true feelings and goals again, defend them, often also fight in order to be victorious.

However, Hollywood itself knows that the hero/heroine has to win in the end – at least something worthwhile for them. How often are we disappointed when a film or book ends negatively. We think to ourselves that we have wasted our time. We tell others that the film or book was bad. It is helpful if we see our own life story, the fairy tale in which we live, exactly this way. It is only in this way that we recognize that we are the authors of our lives. We are never truly dependent.

It is our conditions and demands for external things that make us feel trapped. As such, one of the most popular stories is this: We believe that things would not have been any different, that we have no partner or fulfilling social contacts, that we remained in a job that demoralizes us, or that we are unemployed because... (your story). Even traditional scientists know today that every illness has a history, in which we have unhealthily dealt with ourselves or allowed ourselves to stay in a pathological environment. Things are similar to the fairy tale that we tell ourselves. It is passive when we say that things would not have been any different, we would not have met anyone else, that someone or something is the reason that we are alone and feel lonely, we could not and still cannot do anything, etc. However, we come to decisions in each new minute.

The author Scott Wetzler sums it up as, "They should learn from their mistakes and not live with them for all time." This is because the truth is if we did not do anything and still have not done anything about it, then nothing can change either. Of course, in this case, I am not speaking about traumatic experiences such as existential loss, sexual abuse, or domestic violence. But even codependency in relationships with an alcoholic partner shows that we are and stay there voluntarily.

It is just the same with being alone. Perhaps it may take its time. It was that way for me too. I confess honestly and clearly that little will change quickly if you have stubbornly worked on your fairy tale for a long time. But nothing is as we deceive ourselves to be. Even science has demonstrated that our memories are distorted and are mostly based on the feeling in a situation instead of purely factual events. No one likes to be "at fault". It has nothing to with the question of blame either. We let ourselves be guided by the words in our head and like to believe all our thoughts immediately. Our brain is still an organ that we can control.

The more you dedicate yourself to the origin of the fear, the greater the success. Because with fear, this primal feeling has a right to exist, even if it is sometimes deceitful, like with stress.

TRIGGERS OF FEAR AND LONELINESS

Blame, Shame, and the Need to be Welcome

"Behind every angry soul is a wounded child that just wanted you to love them for who they are."

- Shannon L. Adler

Anxiety and the feeling of loneliness are especially deceiving in conjunction with early experiences that affected us, hurt us, and made us afraid. For our security, our brain memorizes everything that we could need some time. Especially situations where our security was in (apparent) danger.

Beliefs and life patterns

I am on my own. There is no love for me. I am not enough. It is my fault that I am alone. There is something wrong with me!

It is dangerous for a child if their environment seems insecure, if they are torn between their needs and others, if they have no fixed caregiver or have suffered a constant (or one-time) loss of their mother, father, or other family members. As a child, you are totally helpless, have to fend for yourself, and experience helplessness and defenselessness. In addition, children often feel guilty because their parents suffer or have to work because of them, or fight or separate (seemingly) because of them. Typical thoughts include feeling it is their fault if they are neglected, experiencing not enough or no care, or receiving no or too little love and attention. If these thoughts are not rectified, they lead to a sturdy and persistent belief pattern. Therefore, if someone leaves us, physically or emotionally, we believe that it is our fault, that we should have been better, nicer, more well-behaved. We want to be together with people or this particular person. They are not allowed to (in our head) have done something wrong.

Unfortunately, the child within us believes that we still need them today (and in dependent relationships, often decreases the belief in our self-effectiveness). Therefore, we take the responsibility and, often, the blame whenever we are no longer able, allowed to, or supposed to do anything more or they are not there.

Children even learn to suppress and trivialize their anger about their neglect and lack of love.

From these thoughts, a child builds a false conception that he or she always has to look after him or herself so that everyone is okay, he or she is not allowed to cause trouble or is, at best, not even there. Children then simulate their parents, take on their responsibility, attempt to show (the) strength (that adults are supposed to have), and be especially careful in order to avoid feelings of guilt and grief (in adults).

Later in life, this psychodynamics can cause you to always want to have your partner around you in relationships, not want to do anything alone anymore, and to always have to be needed. In turn, others do not get involved with relationships at all anymore in order to not ensure additional weight. However, many develop "being needed" as a basic feeling and need. If they then do not need someone or do not need them any more, a relationship is ended, or friendships, career, or family relations are difficult and in danger, then the old, assumed guilt and old need is reawakened. In doing so, a childlike world remains harmonious and safe.

And in this way, many people put the blame on themselves, willingly bear foreign responsibility and the weight of the burden of their past.

Anger and Fear as Substitute Feelings

However, in the fear of being alone, anger often arises first and foremost. It initially still protects the buried or suppressed sadness. However, when the anger is directed against oneself, it is time to take action. Anxiety, otherwise, forms as a protective mechanism to no longer feel this sadness. Our spirit causes us to try to first and foremost avoid any grief, any fear, and any potential hurt. Our brain controls this in its notorious way. In systemic therapy, we would say, "This is only a failed attempt from the past. We, therefore, need a new one." Our childish solutions for problems are only conditionally effective and can even be harmful.

Life offers many means for avoiding sadness, be it bad relationships, overworking for your career/profession, excessive lifestyles, definition by money and success, as well as alcohol, drugs, tobacco, junk food, excessive sports, sex, etc. To make us feel numb. With this, activities or ways of living become a means of escaping being alone and the sadness associated with it. We learn these ways of compensation throughout our life and usually commit ourselves to one. Many also learn from other people. How Mommy dealt with or reacted to being alone then has an influence.

The questions "What should I do on my own outside then?" or "How should I relax on my own?" are also very familiar for those affected. They feel clueless and empty about the circumstances from which they are rarely able to escape on their own. They think. Many, therefore, hold on to other people, partners, family members, and/or friends and become so dependent on contact so they do not have to face themselves alone.

What Science Believes

Loss and separation at birth do not have anything to do with a (later) fear of being alone. This is what is assumed by many renowned doctors, psychologists, and scientists. It is assumed that even the birth process, that is, leaving the womb, produces a mortal fear in infants. Afterward, later in life, we are constantly left by our attachment figures, be it that our parents go to work or divorce, short-term separations, loss through death, illness, etc. influence us long term. This triggers trauma that rests deep within us but is hopefully resolved later in life. However, with some people, this trauma resurfaces or is, so to speak, triggered through similar moments of loss that remind us of the past. The old fear experienced in the past flares up again to protect us from similarly difficult and menacing feelings.

Well, we may not always be able to find out whenever we have had painful experiences in childhood or youth. Many also remain intentionally blurry, because our brain would never confront us with memories that we could not cope with. It is geared towards protection, even if this is sufficiently proven in many fears.

However, you can try to approach these traumatic experiences cautiously or accompanied by a therapeutically trained person. If this does not work, because you can absolutely not remember, then the first memory in the recent past also helps and, from there, you can jump to the next memory and then another step back. You, therefore, work backward. With heavy trauma, such as sexual abuse or domestic violence, you should exclusively approach these attempts with a therapist.

What is Hidden Behind the Fear of Being Alone?

Many people feel anxiety and sorrow not because they are alone but because they interpret it this way. *I have been/was left alone.* (e.g., in a relationship). This means that they experienced the feeling of loss as a victim-conscious, guilty, passive event coming from outside and caused by external circumstances. They believe the reason for this is they themselves and something "wrong" that they did. It goes hand in hand with a loss of control and of that which provides security. This causes fear, because there are no solutions. Other typical fear patterns include:

The *fear of being idle*. You do not know how to fill idleness, do not feel occupied by others (and/or are hungry for attention), or you are afraid of being busy with yourself instead of with others.

Fear of losing footing when there is nobody nearby. You also sense a general lack of footing in and through yourself.

Fear of being left behind. You fear for yourself when you are alone, only trust other people with difficulty, do not feel in good hands or safe in the world, have the feeling of being important, or even feel a fear of death.

Fear from childhood and the separation from parents and/or other caregivers. Memories of childlike fear of existence trigger the same earlier feelings.

You have a *lack of basic trust* and believe you have no power. You are only able to recognize your own importance and the value you have (also for others) with difficulty. Here, it revolves a lot around a missing independence, interrupted self-development in childhood, frequent consideration for other people, pressure, having to stay a child, and control from other people.

Fear of being recognized in your neediness and weakness. Thoughts about other people's thoughts, possible devaluations, and criticism, vicarious embarrassment and/or being pitied, which reinforce your own feelings, are especially associated with this. These ways of thinking cause people to appear less alone at activities (at the cinema, café, restaurant, etc.) out of fear that others will judge them. External recognition nurtures your self-worth. You only accept yourself when others accept you and only love yourself if a flawless, whole world seems to be there and can be shown – the (illusionistic) whole world of childhood, the security that is maintained when you are *allowed to* be together with and among other people.

With people who have voluntarily entered isolation through this fear because they feel betrayed, abandoned, threatened, or limited by their self-responsibility, you often see the opposite. They leave others and only feel safe inside their own four walls, where the illusion that they are safer indoors can be maintained. These people perhaps experienced external senses of loss in their childhood (suddenly Mom left and was never seen again) or they were often alone in general and waited at home for their parents to come home from work. In secret, they are looking for the safe and sound world of that time again. However, as we are now adults and no form of dependence on our parents exists, we do not live with our parents anymore, a lot of people need a replacement to solve the conflict from that time. For example, a partner or work. These then merely act as a replacement for the attachment figure who we feel left us back then or who did leave us (emotionally, locally, or physically). Loneliness is therefore interpreted as a danger, diffuse independence, sudden and unwanted adulthood, or being left to oneself as if Mommy would say her child, *I'm going now! Take care of yourself.*

The human fear of loss, also in many cases together with the fear of not being needed and having no value for certain people, automatically does this. It is no wonder that many people who are afraid of being alone frequently experience a jump in anxiety: panic attacks, social phobia, generalized fear, agoraphobia, or depression. The fear is then the protection, putting off the transition from dependent to independent, because the child or young person within sits and waits or desires activity and attention. You wait for love and affection. But at the same time, your fear shows you again that this scheme of behavior, playfully trying things out and gathering experiences as children do, may now be initiated. Here, it is like the birth pains, tightness, and fear when transitioning from the safe world to the outer, unfamiliar world to relearn trust and security there.

Many look for this trust and support in a relationship. However, a relationship does not guarantee a lack of loneliness or liberation from anxiety. I address this point in the next chapter. Loneliness despite a relationship and how to overcome it. Those who are not in a relationship can skip this chapter and jump directly to the strategies and methods.

LONELY BUT NOT ALONE

Loneliness in a Relationship

"Loneliness is never more cruel than when it is felt in close propinquity with someone who has ceased to communicate."

Germaine Greer

Sixty percent of all those who complain about being alone and loneliness are married or in a relationship. Although they have a committed partner, they feel abandoned and on the outside. These people have had not felt close contact for a long time: not in conversations, emotionally, or physically. Statistics show that a heavy lack of communication has become a deciding factor in separations and divorces.

How Silence Makes Partners Lonely

Even those who are not married claim to feel alone in relationships. What is missing are conversations that go beyond shopping lists, childcare, household chores, and visits to the in-laws.

The number of minutes in a day that couples spend talking to each other varies greatly. According to a survey[9] carried out in 2010, it was 102 minutes per day, whereby the subjects discussed was not examined. In 2014, a further study showed that as little as 21 minutes of high-quality conversation time per year would be sufficient to feel happy again and to remain so. What positives would appear if you would spare altogether 21 minutes each day out of the average of 15 to 16 hours of waking hours as a couple for each other in addition to the relevant everyday things such as household chores, family occasions, etc.?

Being married or in a relationship does not necessarily prevent feelings of being alone or loneliness. Loneliness is deceptive, as it is only the feeling and not the circumstances that play a crucial role here. Being alone literally means that nobody else is there. But feeling lonely means that you feel alone even if your partner is present.

However, we mix up our feelings when we are lonely. If we have a partner, we unconsciously devalue them and imply to them that they are no longer interested in us or have become less interesting to us. We remove ourselves, because the other has removed themselves from us. While there are people who look for more closeness when they feel distant, right from the same fear, there are those who react more sensitively to

---

[9] Parship 2010

the emotional absence or local separation. You inevitably reach a point where you interpret all signals as negative, for example, as unrequited love or even rejection. People only do this to protect themselves from getting hurt further. When they are already afraid, they protect themselves from further fear.

Unfortunately, this often leads to overlooking the positive, no longer perceiving appreciation but "looking for a fight" as a basic mood. The feelings of the lonely partner are shaped on how the couple's situation looks.

The more everyday things that move in, the more that quality discussions disappear, the more you have gotten to know each other and ended your journey of discovery, the less you concentrate on yourself as a person. While at the beginning of the relationship, you talked about dreams, desires for the future, and important issues, this level fades away more and more. The topics then change over to upbringing, household, or living management. In many cases, this brings human and emotional separation with it. It is also felt in other aspects of cohabitation. While one is watching television downstairs, the other sits upstairs and reads. One partner goes to sleep at 9 p.m., while the other follows two hours later. Cooking and perhaps even eating is done separately, depending on how the living worlds are shaped. Also in relationships without cohabitation or that are not connected by nuptial vows, the difficulty meets reality.

Here, it is easiest for emotionally abusive relationships to be sorted. Where two people who are bad for each other stay together or one partner remains although he or she knows that the relationship is harmful. Emotional abuse refers to actions that evoke emotional pain. The reason for these actions is mostly that the person has been hurt themselves. As such, someone who had been cheated on would also cheat in order to establish an equal footing. Couples would humiliate themselves in front of their children and demand solidarity for one parent. In turn, other partners steer the relationship with lies and manipulation that suit them, forbid feelings, or dispute with the partner.

Whether married or in an unmarried relationship, with children or without, we often prefer to stay with our partner despite all the obstacles and loneliness, instead of leaving. Why? Because we are afraid of being alone. Most accusations between partners who rely on their each other changing something in their behavior to be happy again and for the relationship to work again are based on the fear of being alone. On the one hand, we shun separation and want to hold on to the love and the relationship. On the other hand, the independent mechanisms are disruptive and, all too often, lead to jealousy and hurt. But how can couples find their way back to each other?

Strategies to Experience Relationships Together Again

Take the initiative and stop waiting. Although there may be a fear that the partner is absent, it may be that they are just as lonely as you.[10] In my eyes, only an open and honest discussion between both sides can clear things up and make way for change. Finding the best time for a conversation seems very important to me in this. Those who have caught their partner on the "wrong foot" may get an impression of rejection. You should nevertheless try, because someone has to break through the circle of silence. Use non-violent communication that does not accuse but rather expresses your feelings. Ask about your partner's motivation for their individual behavior. For example, questions that solicit the partner's opinion on something are well-placed. In this way, a respectful eye level can be established.[11]

However, be careful in case a renewed approach is not welcomed immediately in the desired way or euphoria. If something has been prolonged for such a long time, it may also take time to be rectified. Sometimes, a bit of resilience is needed here. And a respectful tone of voice at the right time, not in passing or during times when "a lot is going on".

Have a change of perspective. As difficult as it may be to want to understand the other, it is essential if you want

---

[10] cf. Winch 2013
[11] cf. Winch 2013

to escape the loneliness in your relationship and want to save it. The many questions that we ask internally (Why are you like this again? What did I do? What is wrong with us? What is going on here? Do you still love me? What should I do? What do you expect from me? How can we help ourselves?) must not remain unanswered.

Astoundingly, it is easy to understand the other side whenever you ask them and let them talk without perceiving any word as an offense. Those who are stuck in the spiral of silence will however relate a lot to themselves, potentially misunderstand every word, and interpret it is as criticism or an affront. Perhaps feelings of guilt will surface that will be immediately understood because of the fear of making a mistake. During the conversation, practice understanding everything *neutrally and as information, not an accusation,* with full awareness. Don't just perceive the words but also the feelings at the same time, and yours too. Bring them together to an imaginary film that shows you from the perspective of your partner. Try with all your might to understand him or her. Check everything that has been said as you wish. *Express yourself from your point of view.* Speak with each other peacefully, without accusations and a destructive tone of voice. Share your feelings with each other whenever certain situations or an area of your life are difficult. Both of you should be able to deal with conflict together and solution-oriented. Work out a solution together. How could you find a path and take it so that both of you are content?

Experiences together remain in memory for the longest. However, it is difficult, especially in times when you have removed yourselves from each other, to quickly spend time again completely, authentically, and without problems or distance between each other. Nevertheless, Winch advises taking the step. He believes it is possible to reestablish contact by reminding yourself and your partner of times where you were close and had a true emotional connection with each other. Be it wedding photos and videos, holiday pictures, greeting cards, etc. What once brought you together can bring your together again: children, shared hobbies, new passions, or forgotten dreams that you wanted to realize together.

Ideally, throw all commercial guidebooks in the trash. Look at yourself and your partner individually and not stereotypically. There are dozens of guidebooks on how a man is, how a woman is, how and why they communicate, stay silent, run away, etc. They all have one goal: To attain profit for themselves and/or their publisher. I consider most of these self-help books and expert guidebooks to be truisms and stereotypes. Of course, there are classic schemes of communication and behavior that apply to one or the other person.

And today, there's no end of the "truth" that women always want to talk while men only stay silent or that women always tend towards closeness or control while men want to live out their self-determined and freedom-oriented side. I know quite a few men who do not fit into the hunter behavior and even more women who no longer want to be chased. The times of grouping the sexes together are simply over.

People change when they want to change or have a worthwhile goal in sight that provides them with something profitable. However, since the last century, women have been in a permanent impulse for change, by which I do not only mean in emancipatory or existential matters. They are torn between what they should do and what they want to do, what is enough for them, what they should fight for, what they are able to have, and what they are not. It is similar for men and, in my eyes, sometimes even worse. They are unable to only rely on what the woman shows them. Never have the sexes been so structurally disordered as today. The list of prejudices and emancipatory values is long.

Apart from that, emancipation also applies to men, which many have forgotten today. The classic Marlboro man is just as uncommon as the charming, caring, and selfless angel of the house, as 19th century Victorianism called the ideal women. Nowadays, the sexes are becoming ever closer. Men are becoming softer and women stronger. Men no longer want to have to do so much, while women no longer want to have to do so much and like doing it.

Finally, in relationships, it comes down to just one thing – how do both partners deal with another in dark times? Looking behind the façade is a lot more valuable than any would-be mentor. Instead, care for you and your partner. Refocus on the person in your partner, not the father of your children, the brother of your sister-in-law, the best friend or the entrepreneur, the ideal partner who you thought nothing could ever go wrong with. The same applies to women. The same applies to you. Start with you as a person. This is the only role that needs to be protected. Look behind your façade and be brutally honest with yourself, in what you want, what you long for, what hurts your heart, and what slights your ego. Find out how and what for your feelings and thoughts could be.

Be the change that you want to see in your relationship. That you want a change for your life and so also for your relationship and love together best shows how you yourself want to set things in motion. What is certain, somebody has to take the first step and also show them how to do it if necessary. If we want more time or respect from our partner, we can suggest more activities to them or involve ourselves in theirs. You can kickstart them yourself and also express them in invitations that you wish for your partner to take part.

This can also be implemented regarding behavior. If you want a particular type of behavior from your partner, demonstrate it to them. Ask him or her instead of demanding, ask him or her instead of knowing everything beforehand, talk respectfully with him or her instead of being strict or hurtful. Should these attempts not work, it can still lead to a discussion about why the partner is not interested. At the very least, you have effected a change for yourself.

It can only be positive for you yourself when you take your life into your own hands and lead it towards your goal on your own, in spite of a relationship. Do things with yourself, and then your partner will be sure to want to take part. He or she will at least notice that you are doing something for yourself. This is always attractive and shows that you are active. It is very likely that he or she will compare your behavior with his or hers. The results will fall into place. This method could be good for those who believe in the law of attraction. Because primarily only demanding and being correspondingly disappointed when the expectations remain unmet can become very frustrating for both partners.

BRING THE SELF-CONFIDENCE AND
SELF-LOVE HERE!

Strategies and Methods for the Advanced

Tip 1: The step-by-step method

Those who especially need the closeness of a certain person or can barely manage without them can try a *step-by-step withdrawal program* with them. You discuss the procedure and the goal and explain to the person who is present beside you as an observer that you would like to learn to be alone in one-minute increments. Expressing this goal clearly is encouraging even if it is scary.

Minute for minute, you plan a step-by-step plan for solitude with a set list of activities that you do in the meantime and *which are important to you* (no social media, forums, or indirect exchange opportunities). The partner or attachment figure then agrees that you will intentionally be left alone by them so that you safely learn how to be alone in the confrontation.

You can start small on day 1 so that you set aside five minutes in the morning and 10 minutes in the evening for alone time. The support consists of you being able to call the observer at any time or go/drive to them. After the time runs out, you discuss your feelings with the person and change the processes according to your own need. On day 2, the minutes are doubled. In turn, you discuss how you felt. On the following day, you can incorporate a greater time jump or stay with doubling the time.

You carry on with this method until you feel good and secure on your own. Through the support and the chance to stop at any time, it is a guarantee that this leap into the water is not too cold at all.

Tip 2: Ways of compensating for inner footing

Instead of surrounding yourself with people and nurturing yourself with their closeness and attention, you can learn afresh to enrich yourself with activities that bring you joy.

In addition to the "normal" activities, which I am also listing for the sake of completeness, I will present many strategies in the following that come from life coaching and my imagination from the time of my anxiety and loneliness.

Exercise – done differently

Light sports, e.g. jogging, Pilates, stretching, and yoga, encourage inner serenity and give you the feeling that you have achieved something by yourself and on your own. Yin Yoga, in particular, is a sure guarantee of inner peace. You have to engage yourself in it as the exercises in Yin Yoga are held for three minutes. At the end, relaxation and carefreeness are certain.

It is similar with relaxation techniques such as progressive muscle relation, which breaks down aggression, anxiety, panic, and depressive moods in the short term. Watch some excellent instruction videos on YouTube and copy them directly. Autogenic training also makes it possible to immediately interrupt yourself in all negative thoughts.

Those who prefer sitting activities may of course watch television, whereby research has sufficiently proven that it needs to deal with positive issues in order to not bring the mood back down. Those who are used to watching detective series, thrillers, horror, dramas, the news, and other disturbing, frightening, or intellectually *exciting* shows should therefore try something with light and cheery content such as romance films, comedies, fairy tales, sports films, etc.

Doing sport has also proven to have mentally uplifting effects. For this reason, sports therapy and psychotherapy are becoming more and more united. They are on the order of the day at clinics. However, sports can even work wonders for those who do not yet feel completely excessive demands. This is because doing sports lowers the secretion rate of stress hormones such as cortisol and noradrenaline. We all know that stress makes you ill. The life expectancy of mentally ill people is therefore on average up to 20 years less than that of healthy people. But sports causes endorphins, happiness hormones, to be secreted. Doctor Bente Pedersen discovered that working muscles also cause the secretion of so-called myokine, healing messenger substances. Today, they are considered the sole cause for sports being so effective with and against illnesses. Meanwhile, it is also clear that an endogenous fear inhibitor, the peptide ANP, is released during sports. A Dutch study from 2011 showed that just 60 minutes of sports per week lowered the risk of depression, anxiety and panic disorders, and addictions. The recovery also takes place a lot faster if those affected regularly do sports.

Sports has an opposite effect on self-effectiveness and feelings such as inferiority, helplessness, defenselessness, and sadness. Those who manage to get back on their feet feel that they are more capable of action. Feeling small, worthless, and victimized is lowered. With it, doing sports even strengthens confidence and self-awareness and promotes resilience.

Sports also gives you the ability to endure burdensome circumstances, feats, and crises. Then our head knows that the body can withstand longer periods of stress without any danger. In times of heavy strain and mental issues, however, we tend to think that we are no longer able to endure anything and afford anymore. In fact, through regular sport, the mind is taught that it can "press" through and "carry" a certain amount and that it has more "endurance" and "strength" than previously thought.

Sports is also one of the best methods for setting broodings and worries aside. Those who burn off energy physically know that there is no time or room in the meantime to think about the problems of life intensely and full of anxiety. You are too preoccupied with your body: breathing, keeping up, straining the individual muscle groups. Instead, doing sports forces the brain to make room. Those who think nevertheless about the challenges of their life during sports ensure that the stress level from worrying will immediately be reduced again. They simply get rid of their stress and worries through sports. Moving while brooding is therefore the best thing that you can do. It resulted in US-American scientists always advising to reach for the vacuum cleaner and cloth in an emergency if there was no time left for other sports.

Physical agitation, exertion, and entire physical or somatic pains are also lowered through doing sports. Short kickboxing sessions or jogging can work wonders with fear and panic because they break down stress reactions on a physical level. In this way, you reduce weak knees, dull sensations in your limbs, the lump in the throat, powerlessness, palpitations, breathing difficulties, sensitivity to bright light and loud noises, circulatory problems in heat, and much more.

People with depression and phobias do particularly little sports, which goes hand in hand with panic attacks. Unfortunately, this leads to even short sports sessions or exertion overwhelming the body. Becoming more hardened by building up fitness step by step, therefore, helps against the symptoms, hypochondria, cardiac neurosis, and the fear of the fear.

In addition, endurance sports, such as jogging, cycling, swimming, and walking, should help with phobias, anxiety states, panic attacks, and depression. A Norwegian study also showed that especially Asian martial arts help with depression, for example:

- Karate
- Ki-Aikido
- Jiu Jitsu
- Judo
- Kendo
- Nam Hong Son
- Sumo
- Tai Chi
- Wing Chun
- Wing Tsun
- Wushu and much more.

It is however crucial that you choose a type of sport that you enjoy. Doing sports in regular intervals then works like psychotherapy. Those who practice sports with compulsion and irritation would not profit from the positive effects. If you prefer weight training, do not toil away at jogging. If you prefer team sports, take a closer look at ball sports. Boxing and squash against aggressions just like martial arts are also worth taking a look at for more self-confidence. Yoga (especially Yin Yoga), Tai Chi, and Qi Gong are worthwhile for those who want to promote a greater level of inner peace. Anyone who generally has too little time for sports or does not want to use their free time to partake in it should try out the small art of HIIT (High-Intensity Interval Training). There are numerous phone apps that can achieve the desired effect in less than 10 minutes.

Unconditional friends

Play with animals/children. This stirs up cuteness and is proven to cause the secretion of the happiness hormone serotonin. Especially animals whom we associate with emotionally joyful experiences help you to feel less lonely but more relaxed. As such, cats are rather more ideal for introverted, affectionate people. Dogs are more for extroverted people or those who want contacts that they can find easily when out walking the dog. Horses are particularly meaningful because they represent freedom and the desire for distance, experiments, adventure, and the zest for life. Whichever animal you decide on, animals are usually unconditional and will always love you, no matter what circumstances take over your life.

The classics

These activities have proven to be particularly effective in combination with spiritual relaxation: reading, writing, painting, singing, crafting, handicrafts, gardening, and playing instruments. All of these inspire the imagination and open the door to areas of the subconscious. Reading and painting have proven to be especially good at relieving fear and brightening moods. At any rate, in art and music therapy, they are found in abundance in the struggle against fears (phobias), depression, and other imbalances.

In the following chapter, I would like to take a closer look at singing and humming as another option, because using one's own voice has proven to have healing effects beyond monolog speaking. It is also a good companion with acute anxiety.

Tip 3: Your voice against fear and sorrow

If your own voice (in both the figurative and literal sense) is muted or too quiet to be heard or you do not trust yourself to raise it, other ways of *speaking out* must be found. Because *from the pressure* of the feelings that are suppressed or hidden, comes stress, grief, fear, and panic. Circles of thoughts, broodings, self-condemnation/guilt, self-degrading. *Hey, but I'm worth something!* says this quiet voice of panic that the other (foreign) voices want to drown out but that needs us and our body to do something against the circumstances. Your feelings need you! YOU. Stress is the first sign of this. Therefore, in my own times of panic, I invented a method that I still apply in difficult phases today. These methods make it possible,

a) to use your voice,
b) to generate positive feelings,
c) to express yourself, and
d) to bring yourself out of your broodings.

Areas of application

- Use always, when broodings about irritating or frightening situations/people start in the head or are simply difficult to stop.
- During stress, strains, anxiety, or increasing panic.
- Whenever you are outside and have to put up with too much noise, people, and other things (sensory overload).
- When you feel alone/lonely.

Procedure

Choose a children's song from early days or a favorite song that is associated with a POSITIVE situation. In thinking of the chosen song, you should automatically feel safe and secure. If you have chosen a song, every time your brooding concert sets in, you can start your own by humming this song. You can hum quietly or more loudly, depending on where you are and how much "noise" you trust yourself to make.

Variations

There are people, and you are sure to know a few of them, who stroll through the street or sit next to you on the bus whistling, singing, or talking on the phone. This is that one extreme. The other extreme is people who stand quietly next to you, feeling annoyed, barely coping with their feelings about this "burden", or simply not being able to contain themselves, staring at someone in the hope that they notice it on their own.

And in between these is humming. It can be controlled. You decide whether everybody notices it or nobody does. You can hum quietly as well as loudly. You can hum with your voice as well as your breath. Try out all these humming options once in order to find your favorite:

a. Humming and your voice is loudly audible.
b. Humming with your breath: You only awaken the feeling of humming but you are only using your vocal cords and causing them to sound/vibrate.
c. Humming quietly.

Variation 1 can be used anywhere where you can be loud, e.g. at home, in the fresh air, on the go, with a lot of background noise. Variation 2 can be used anywhere where you would like to attract less attention, e.g. in the supermarket, at a meeting, in a line. Variation 3 is for places where there is light background noise, e.g. on the bus, railway, tram, or train.

Why hum?

1. Humming, therefore activating your voice, activates you. It centers you, brings mindfulness, and leads you to concentrate on yourself. It also brings you away from other people or background noises. Those who suffer seemingly dangerous physical reactions, such as irregular heartbeat and palpitations, sweaty hands, muscle tension, weak knees, tightness in the chest, difficulty swallowing, etc., can find peace again using this technique.
2. It keeps your concentration on yourself for the length of the hummed song, instead of being distracted again by a carousel of broodings.
3. It strengthens self-confidence, because using *your own voice* is a crucial element in self-healing. You hear yourself, you notice, *there is a 'me'. I am.*
4. It activates self-control and self-effectiveness. *I can express myself. I decide when I speak and how.*
5. It activates proper breathing. In typical anxiety and panic breathing, the person tries to inhale as much air as possible, while exhalation is shortened. We retain more carbon dioxide and struggle to breathe. This makes the symptoms tremendously worse. But if we hum, sing, or speak, then we have to breathe out. We have no other choice.

De-**sense**-ing

I invented the method of de-sense-ing as an addition. Close your eyes, shut your ears, but the main thing is to *always open one* main sense.

With fear and panic, you have a low stimulus threshold or your sensitivity to a fast and intense sensory overload is high. This can be reduced by de-sense-ing. Whenever you hum on your way to the mailbox or subway, stand and hum in the line at the supermarket, close your eyes and block out all visual stimuli that would otherwise come under your radar. The concentration only rests on the acoustic signals. Whenever you then open your eyes again, concentrate exclusively on the acoustic, on your ears, and perceive them more predominantly than the visuals.

It works exactly the same the other way around. Close your ears (or do as if you had an earache and shut your ear muscles with your hands). Ideally, lower your head when you do this and briefly isolate yourself visually from your environment in order to focus your sight. Whenever you raise your head again, block out all noises that are still partially there from your concentration. Only perceive what is visual. Whenever you then "re-open" your ears, focus only on what you see.

Anyone can try it out for themselves what is more effective. You can basically find out which of your senses is stronger and what your ideal learning style would be by taking a simple test that comes from learning coaching.

The senses test

Close your eyes and imagine you are at the ocean. It is a wonderful day, you feel good. What do you notice first? The sand under your foot? The wind on your skin? The salt on your tongue? Do you see the ocean and the waves first? Or do you hear them first?

Assessment

If you feel the sand under your feet, this indicates that haptics is your dominant channel. You are therefore a touch and feel person and need contact through your body. If you hear the ocean, it is your acoustic channel that is more pronounced. If you see it, you are a visual person. If you smell the ocean or the air, your olfactory senses are in the foreground. If you taste salt or seafood, it is the so-called gustatory sense that is more prominent for you.

You can find your first and second senses that are most developed and either block out both when you are coming into a situation of anxiety and panic or consciously activate and focus on one of them while the other is blocked out.

It is and remains important that you take responsibility for yourself within instead of waiting for attention from outside or even to exist. Learning to occupy yourself alone and enjoy doing so leads to a better, more balanced life in the long term, which will also benefit your relationships. Especially your relationship with yourself.

Tip 4: Build closeness to yourself

How can you become close with yourself? Psychology knows many techniques for building closeness with oneself and strengthening yourself internally:

Writing therapy

As early as ancient times, writing has been considered an effective way of relieving negative thoughts and feelings, because we integrate the fear back as an *accepted part of our personality*. Recognizing it as a separate element that rules over us, on the other hand, paralyzes our action. Regarding stress and fear as a part of us and working with it, dedicating a space and time to write, making it more transparent for us, relieves its existence. It allows people who write to find out more about themselves and their feeling, while at the same time, express it. Otherwise, the counter-effect would be called:

- ignoring yourself,
- being afraid of your feelings,
- wanting to inhibit your feelings.

Have you ever tried to ban yourself from stress and sudden fear in the sense of sweaty hands, palpitations, blushing, or panic? Exactly, it simply doesn't work. In our brain, we have an area where recognition or rejection is transmitted directly to the fear center so that our fear is fed. But first, we make a decision about it. We either decide for or against fear, for or against worrying and brooding, for or against panic attacks. This decision is partially taken away from us when we consciously or unconsciously know, *in such moments, I was often afraid.* The memory of it creates a new decision. In these new moments, we would have to directly intervene and say, *I used to be afraid in these moments, but today I am deciding against it and instead for confidence.* However, we mistakenly believe that an external factor would make a choice against us. Fortunately, the human brain is able to interrupt its chain of thoughts and feelings, in which we as people transform the frightening feelings.

Writing from a psychological point of view

Writing is one of the oldest forms of self-communication, self-help, and self-healing. Even back in 500 B.C., philosophers, such as Socrates and Plato in Greece, began to use writing for human fates and feelings, as well as self-coaching. The Roman philosophers used writing as a form of self-criticism; the Stoics used it to concentrate and to meditate. All of them explored their true self through writing, as a self-analysis, self-awareness, and self-recognition. The famous philosophers Kant, Hegel, and Descartes used writing to oppose values, confront them, and, at the same time, find their own role in society in order to relieve their suffering under the dominant morals and self-doubt.

They brought the famous form of self-healing, the diary, into the world. They invented writing as a safe place, an individual place of retreat. The theologist Augustinus developed the autobiographical diary from which the autobiography came. The well-known automatic writing also developed in psychological directions and in mystic circles. The author Sylvia Winnewisser[12] describes a story, which says that the first person who used writing as a kind of healing from their troubles and problems, broodings and harmful illusions (i.e., fear) was a certain Daniel Paul Schreber, who healed himself from these negative feelings – using writing. This was at the beginning of the 20th century.

Modern times have certainly not become easier. This is why we need access to ourselves, a possibility of being able to heal and free ourselves from everything on our own. In doing so, we can learn from the past and harness an ancient means: Writing.

According to renowned psychologist Verena Kast, fears are only an unpleasant term for worries, strains, stress, and blockades. For example, irritation and anger are wholly human defense mechanisms from fear. Nobody wants to have or feel anxiety. But somehow everybody has to deal with everyday stress, problems in career or relationships, blockades in upcoming or necessary changes. All of us constantly feel anger and irritation

---

[12] cf. Winnewisser 2010

at our fellow humans, at ourselves, or about situations and circumstances that we cannot change and have to accept and survive. Writing catches hold of these negative thoughts and works with them.

10 reasons to use writing against fear

1. Writing is possible from anywhere, be it shortly before the terrifying exam, on the bus during anxiety or panic attacks, or at night in bed, when you are unable to sleep because your thoughts are running in circles.
2. Writing is cost-efficient. All that you need is a pen and paper.
3. Writing is healing. You free yourself from all the negative and troublesome feelings. Science has proven that writing, so to speak, empties out the areas of the brain that start with negative thoughts and trigger negative feelings. When writing, you clear space in your head as if you are taking out the trash.
4. Writing is a safe space for anyone, especially for those who find it difficult to open themselves up to someone or to reveal their thoughts and feelings. Paper doesn't judge. It allows you to be as you are and want to be.
5. What you write remains. Both lovely and sad experiences, important events that you want to read about later such as how you felt in a situation, what you want to say to someone – you hold onto everything in writing. Nothing is forgotten. You remain

because you write. You can also write in public places and distract yourself from the hustle and bustle around you. I always did it whenever I knew that I might have a panic attack. I wrote and my fear stayed away.

6. Everything that you do not dare to feel, you can still write down. It is not just about not wanting to trust a person with something. We are often our biggest critics and deny ourselves feelings and thoughts because we do not believe we are allowed to have them. On paper, even the darkest shades of ourselves are permitted.
7. You learn about yourself. You will notice that sudden thoughts, which you were not at all aware of, come to mind. This is not just interesting – it gives you space to get to know yourself and to grow.
8. Everyone has something inside of them that tells them that they are worth loving and a caring person. This is still true. It is often other people who blame and weigh us down with their values and demands. In writing, you can liberate yourself from this and learn to understand yourself and other people better.
9. You redevelop a closeness with yourself, especially if you are someone who often does a lot for others, often neglecting or even forgetting yourself in the process. In this case, you should write to reestablish contact with yourself and your needs.

10. Writing, therefore, unloads in the short term, middle term, and long term. Instead, the brain creates new space for new experiences. In writing, your own control and solution orientation return to you. You develop ideas and experience your daydreams, the small and great wishes jump onto the paper and suddenly you realize, Hey, that's me.

Exercises from writing therapy

In the following, I would like to offer several exercises from writing therapy that are easy to carry out and very liberating.

- writing a letter to yourself or your anxiety,
- writing out your thoughts in a journal,
- start a gratitude journal,
- write a letter to someone who you consider responsible or hurtful from your point of view. Then write yourself a reply from the point of view of the person, putting yourself in this person's position. Finally, write a third, neutral letter, from the view of yourself when you are 20 or 40 years older and have gained some distance from the situation.

Streams or Yin Shin Jyutsu

Some people call it healing hands or impulse streams, others only streams, others, in turn, the laying on of hands, and the old Japanese art of healing calls it Jin Shin Jyutsu, after Jiro Murai. These belief systems and disciplines have one thing in common, they use the hands and the energy to heal themselves and others, reduce physical problems, and trigger thought patterns through healing touches or blockades. In Austria, it is even recognized by health insurance companies as a method. However, strictly speaking for these streams, you need a hand and no doctor, healer, or other healing person to help you. Every classic treatment is unnecessary. You don't even need the gift of healing. In streams, we only work with our own energy. Whether you are currently going through a period of self-doubt or are doing well plays no role. The healing energy is within you, no matter what your ego tells you.

It struck me how obviously we use our hands for comfort in everyday life, usually for others:

- You place your hand on someone's shoulder and show them: I am feeling with you.
- You place your hand on someone's back and show them: I am strengthening you. I have your back.
- You place your hand in the nape of your neck and on your shoulder when you are tense in order to bring about relaxation.

- With your partner, you unconsciously place your hand on their chest (the heart region) and show them: I love you. I am giving your love. I am filling your heart.
- We caress dear people and show them: I am with you. You mean a lot to me. I want to be close to you.
- We stroke animals and children and show them: You are adorable, cute, kind, valuable.
- We reach out our hand to someone to support them and to show them: You are not alone.
- We shake hands to show someone: I appreciate you.

You see, your hands are used everywhere, even unconsciously, whenever we give, need, or feel love. You can use this approach for yourself, because "When the hands are busy, the mind is silent and warm hands warm the soul." Another Russian proverb says, *"The hands create happiness and drive away sorrow."* If you can love yourself, you can also heal yourself.

Whenever I remember my anxious times when I was doing badly, where I was racked with every worry that prevented sleep and caused headaches or stomach aches, I unconsciously and intuitively placed my hand on the place from a certain point in time – whether it was on my head, which was rattling because I was frantically looking for solutions and running through potential scenarios, or on pains in my body, where I placed my hand on my stomach or in the nape of my neck or, in times of fear, on my heart. All of this made me feel better, as anyone would do when they feel pain. We automatically place our hand on the painful place. The thought occurred to me – what would happen if we consciously carried out this automatism and for a longer period? I did not know that there were already methods that intensely dealt with making it into its own art. However, these can also be used for healing yourself. You do not need any third party. You are your own healer.

I coincidentally read in a book that you can bring about peace by using lavender oil and rubbing it on your heart. Through the pleasant warmth in the heart region, it promotes relaxation and inner peace. When I told a friend who works as a physiotherapist this, she flatly said, "So, touching yourself, of course!" Another friend knew the streams from her grandmother who always encouraged her to try them out.

How streams are carried out

By laying our hands on certain regions of our body, we can relieve pain using our own energy. In Jin Shin Jyutsu, for example, you start from 26 "energy locks", or positions in the body, which can be activated through hand contact. Positive emotions can also be triggered by so-called finger streams, a less conspicuous variation for in public. This method can be used everywhere, anywhere, and is free – on the bus, on the train, while waiting in line, at the cinema, during a meeting, or wherever else. You could say that you use your own self-healing powers and, in doing so, get blocked energy "flowing" again. Blockades created by emotions, such as annoyance, sadness, anger, or fear, can be resolved in this way. But our environment also affects our body, our energy, or our lack of energy. Whenever you go over displeased, mild depressive, or depressed phrases and the emptiness connected with it, you can view streams as a method of refilling yourself. With our own physical energy that (still) lies dormant within us.

In the process, the following thinking patterns or feelings are assigned to a different finger and can be balanced out through streams:

> *Thumbs with worries*: You enclose your left thumb with your right palm (as if you want to pull at it). Your right thumb can point upwards or downwards, as you choose. You hold it until you feel balance.
> *Index finger with fear*: Same procedure, only with the left index finger.
> *Middle finger with anger and annoyance*: Same procedure, only with the left middle finger.
> *Ring finger with sadness and distress*: Same procedure, only with the left ring finger.
> *Little finger with lack of love and joylessness*: Same procedure, only with the left little finger.
> *Palms with lacking self-confidence*: Lightly press the left palm with the right thumb or hold it with the whole hand (like with hand holding).

This technique helps against broodings, battered self-esteem, inner emptiness, tension headaches, and panic. As I have already mentioned, you can use streams with insomnia in order to switch off broodings, worries, or sadness. You simply place one hand on your head and the other on a part of your body that feels okay. The overload is balanced through the other places. This can also be done with the heart. Place your hand on your heart and calmly breathe in and out. If you like, imagine the energy in your hand is streaming into your heart and is helping you.

The inner child

Encouraging the child within, the hurt part of your personality, and calming it allows you to accept old fears. As if you were speaking to your own frightened child, you explain to them that you are safe. You carry out a mental or spoken conversation with them. If you have trouble remembering yourself as a child, photos or objects from that time may help you connect with your childhood. You can ask the child within what it is afraid of, how it feels, and welcome the answers openheartedly and warmly from the adult point of view. Likewise, you can explain to them that their feelings are okay but, in the moment, everything is safe. The adult part must stand up for the child-self. This conversation is about lovingly accepting their doubts and fears, not obedience.

A wonderful form of appreciation is a method from writing therapy that I briefly outlined in the relevant chapter: Writing letters. It perhaps seems strange that you dedicate a letter to your inner child, the little nipper who once were. Nonetheless, it can be wonderful and helpful to spend time with them. An encouraging and comforting example from me is this letter:

My little, stubborn, lively, sad, curious, bubbly, playful sweetheart,

There will be people who see the world with different eyes to yours and make fun of and reject you and your values and make them out to be unreasonable. Despite this, stay true to yourself and hold on tight to what you believe. You are just as important as they are.

There will be people who trigger helplessness and weaknesses in you with their words and actions, who play with their power and would run down anyone – not just you – just to be at the top. They are afraid of falling behind. Stay strong and let them go their way, even when you do not understand it.

There will be situations that you didn't see coming. This is exactly when you should watch out for and stick by yourself, loving yourself as you are and remembering what you are worth. Everything passes, sooner or later. Every thought passes by. No pain lasts forever.

There will always – no exceptions – be a solution for every problem. Even if these solutions are not what you would have wanted. At the end of the day, everyone will have and get what they need and deserve. If necessary, even a wake-up lesson.

There will be people whose possessions and respect is more important than anything else. Perhaps they will try to buy you or impress you with what they have. Perhaps they will even expect you to be nicer to them – love them – because you are impressed by their possessions and image. Make your own decisions regardless of this, let them go their way, and refocus on your value.

There will be people who leave you, even if you have not changed or nothing has happened. Forgive them and relate it only to them and their dreams. Your value remains the same.

There will be people who leave you, because you changed or want to change. Forgive them and relate it only to them and their desires. Your journey remains the same. Do not be held back by others' fears or desires. Many relationships will only serve for a certain time.

There will be people who you hurt through your actions and words. Remind yourself that these people and relationships are living and cannot only be hurt but also healed from their pain again. Take the first step.

There will people who are unable to apologize for their mistakes or say thanks. For nothing or no one. They cannot do anything else. It means something to them to be this way and not be any different. It is their form of protection. They are unable to carry any more guilt. They already have – even if you do not see it – enough on their shoulders. It is pointless to question others' behavior. They will know what they are doing and what for.

Do not try to understand the mind of other people just because they turn their back on you. Don't ask yourself why someone does or leaves something. Do not invade their thoughts or question their feelings. If they want to disclose something to you, they will do it. If they do not share anything with you, then it's because they don't want to.

Never try to convince anyone that you are worth loving. Either the person will see it themselves and love you or they won't see it and won't love you. That's why being sad wastes your time with those who are ready and willing to accept and like you as you are.

Always get back up when you fall. There are some stones that you miss and some mountains that you wrongly believe you can conquer. Don't be ashamed of trying. Instead, shrug your shoulders and find out what happened so that you can avoid it next time. Try it out, but never give up. Always keep going. It is the only way that you will reach your goal.

Be good to yourself and your body, not only when you are sick. Look after yourself, even on healthy days. Learn the measure of all things and never deliberately hurt your body. It gives you a home for your life on earth. When your house is broken, your life will not be worth living.

Try to forgive all the people who have hurt you, including yourself. They could not do anything else. They were caught in themselves. They were afraid. They had a different way before them. If you hurt someone, recognize it and apologize if you still can. The more liberated you are from your actions and their consequences, the freer and more independent you will be able to be in the future.

Make strong connections. Don't be afraid of getting hurt. Do not shy away from expressing your feelings.

Love with all your heart even if it turns out to be a mistake afterward. Those will be the days that you remember later. That is how you will be remembered.

Be unconditional, but not naive. Love with the heart of a child but the sense of an adult. Skip around like a child, but pursue your goal like an adult.

Maintain your lightness, joy, and longing, but use it directly for the greater good in which you live.

Always preserve the interests of the community. If they no longer fit your own, make sure that someone else preserves them in your place and take a new path with a new community. Get involved in every group with your many ideas and emotions. Give something of your ability. Only in this way will you grow and find people that are suited to you.

Last but not least, there will be times that are there for solitude in order to return to yourself and regather strength. But also remember that people are not made for loneliness. Whichever reasons you will have for being alone or not alone, make sure that you are always in the right place at the right time. Every situation is made for you to help you grow more and learn to understand yourself. Always show sympathy for yourself. This is your only shield of protection in all the times that are still difficult. But know, too, that every period of grief and pain must give way to the life in you at some point.

Accept death, but choose life. Use it as well as possible as long as you live.

*Sincerely,
Your adult Janett!*

Such letters or words in themselves can provide valuable insights into the dynamics of the fear of being alone. Every person feels alone or even lonely from time to time. The difference is how you value the time for you alone. If you experienced time alone as negative and frightening in the past, our brain offers a new chance of remembering how you felt back then in order to work through it. If the brain was not ready to start making this change, then it would not confront you with it.

Tip 5: What would you have to do for things to get worse?

If it hurts really bad or you are infuriated, have anxiety or panic attacks, or cry yourself to sleep, ask yourself what you have to do for it to get even worse:

- Torture yourself more by degrading yourself?
- Treating yourself even more unkindly and worthlessly so that you feel unloved and worthless?
- Sleep even less, eat even more, be around people less often, drink even more?

Your brain is a powerful organ and, as always, it will do what it has to in order to maintain functionality in your life. It will protect you and pull you from the swamp. Whether it is through aha moments, new force pulses, or help that you accept or look for. The first step is observing yourself and the critics.

What can you do instead that would be helpful and support you in your self-worth, self-acceptance, and self-love? Introducing small rituals into your everyday life, such as cooking your favorite food, taking an adult evening course, exploring a new place in your area that only you visit and which is not associated with any memories, can be just as helpful as the first impulses that come into your head when you ask yourself, "What can I do to feel better?"

Tip 6: Let your "real" feelings out

In non-violent communication, we differentiate between real and unreal feelings. Real feelings are sadness, annoyance, insult, helplessness, fear, loneliness, boredom, disappointment, jealousy, and emptiness. Unreal feelings are "constructed". They don't come from your heart but rather stem from your mind. You feel like you think, for example:

- rejected
- used
- lied to or cheated
- despised
- humiliated
- abandoned
- ignored
- overlooked
- insignificant
- neglected
- dismissed
- unwanted
- worthless
- unloved.

Make it clear to yourself when they arise, that you are not feeling these constructed, unreal feelings at all. They are your thoughts, your interpretations. The sources are unrequited feelings and a desire for love. These unreal feelings reflect your fear. In turn, they protect you from too much sorrow, which your brain does not want to feel. It is a little as if your brain was allowing you to develop an individual anger or something different and greater, which then gives you the ability to take a new path. For some people, this can mean that they try and do even more in order to convince somebody that they are worth something and worth loving. In turn, people decide to reject others because they feel rejected by others. On the other hand, real feelings include self-sympathy and the belief in the hope of a better future.

Tip 7: Look in the mirror and recognize yourself in it

Stand in front of a mirror and look at yourself. See yourself, not just someone in your head that you talk to, discuss with, or miss. Look in the mirror. That is you. This is how you look when you feel these feelings or have these thoughts that you are having. Do you like yourself like this? Can you sympathize with yourself or do you feel rather self-pity? Or do you see yourself as you are? Do you look like how others see you or how you want to be seen or do you allow yourself an honest look into the mirror that shows you that you have rough edges that are a part of you? What you think and feel about yourself is your decision. Whenever you allow someone else to define your values and untruths about your person, you will become a different person, someone who tries to squeeze a circle that is too big into a square that is too small. However, who are you without the others?

Tip 8: Feel the pain that you want to process

The psychologist and author Chuck Spezzano once said that it is the pain we take back into our lives that we most want to let go of inside: old sorrow about separations, abandonment, sacrifice, conflicts, rejection whether on the part of the mother, father, old friends, or partner. This, in connection with a guilt that you feel, which is not necessarily your own but can be also someone else's, causes us to partly suffer for decades. While we are angry and sad, the person we blame does not apologize and also does not make up for their guilt. Instead, they are cold, self-important, and completely convinced by their opinion and behavior, which hurts us even more.

This old pain is reactivated every time because it is still there and lives in us like a sleeping dog, whenever someone similar or with similar characteristics comes into our lives. You draw comparisons, know that you already experienced "something like this", and go through the same thing as in the past, only more painfully. The goal behind this is to endure this pain – as long and as often as it needs until we are ready – in order to finally be able to let it go. Also, the guilt that somebody did not want to accept or the responsibility that someone did not want to carry reverts to us, because we cannot let it go and we accept it for the other person. In their position, we behave the way we expected and hoped for from the other person and we especially try to make up for the foreign guilt. But in doing so, we forget that our anger and sadness remain hidden in order to not have to feel the pain. The pain will be there until you are ready to feel and process it, by admitting it. You are innocent.

Tip 9: Forgive your feelings

It is not a crime, but rather the most human thing, to be needy (read: have needs). It is normal that it hurts when these needs are unfulfilled or remain for a longer period of time. Suppressing them or blaming ourselves for it will however only cause them to want to surface even more. Most psychological growths are only able to arise, because we suppress our needs and feelings about them. Marshall Rosenberg, the founder of non-violent communication, once said, "Behind every uncomfortable feeling lies an unfulfilled need." Since there are no pills and remedies for loneliness, you can only try one thing – accept that you long for contact and recognition, that you sometimes feel rejected and talk yourself into the mindset that that has a meaning and a reason. Forgive your feelings and, above all, allow yourself to feel them. Furthermore, ask yourself the following questions:

- What do you need to feel accepted?
- Do you need certain people or just anyone?
- Why (reason) and what is it for (purpose)?

- Do you need the feelings of others in order to feel good?
- How do you feel about others?
- How do you feel about yourself and your situation?
- What would you advise yourself – in my position?
- Who are you without the others?

The answers to these questions may help you to uncover the true reasons for your way of thinking. Then see what happens to you when you simply leave the feelings and needs be – without evaluations, additional thoughts or broodings, or objective planning.

Tip 10: Fall in love again – this time with yourself

Would you like to marry yourself? Would you enjoy being together with somebody like you? Would you love somebody who is exactly like you? If not, then perhaps you have become a better version of a person that others would consider worth loving. Out of the fear of rejection. *Would you love somebody with your qualities?* These are the exact uncomfortable questions that should reveal to you whether you have become caught in someone else's narrow universe. Free yourself from it. Set the thoughts and demands of other people aside.

Take a pen and paper and note down the qualities that you find positive and attractive in others. Then write down those that you find repulsive and questionable. Now take a look at the list from these perspectives. Which of the positive traits do you have? Which of the negative traits do you find again in some areas of your life? How can you integrate the positive characteristics that you (still) lack? What can you do against the negative ones? Which of the negative qualities are *really* negative? Where do the values for "positive" and "negative" come from? Do they originate from other people?

Go back to the first chapter where you listed your qualities and the thankful aspects of your personality and your life. Always remember these and learn afresh each day that what you think about yourself counts. This is because these thoughts shape your feelings. As such, "only" solitude can come from loneliness again, and from that "only" boredom. The allows you to go backward and discard your previous misconceived thoughts.

Tip 11: Recognize that you get what you want in order to learn something

During a time when relationships were not going well for me, I found a German book with the title *Jeder bekommt den Partner, den er verdient – ob er will oder nicht* (*Everybody gets the partner they deserve – whether they want to or not*) by Hermann Meyer. I was shocked by his statements and couldn't believe what the author was delivering as arguments. Should it really be my "fault" that things went so wrong with this partner? Was my choice of partner unconscious? Had I intentionally chosen a person for myself who dealt with me (and themselves) negligently? Yes. I did want him. I ignored all the signs and, today, I am certain that it was purely intentional and, above all, an insight that I wanted to get. But right to the end I firmly believed that it would one day be the most wonderful relationship in my life, with adorable children and happiness and a house and a dog and a garden, at the end of a meadow full of daisies. Today, I know better.

Very often we get what we give and receive what we believe we "deserve", because it fully corresponds to the opportunities we have in that moment (whether consciously or unconsciously). Do you believe, like I did many years ago, that you would have to achieve a lot to *earn love* in the truest sense of the word?

If you were a friend of mine, you would surely just shake your head and appeal to my conscience, right?

- Who are you as a partner?
- What do you believe you deserve?
- What is the worst thing that was ever suggested to you and what did you do in that moment?
- Gave more, stayed silent, tried, suffered?

Then it seems like you believe that you have earned this behavior and such a partner. Or you shook your head and went and found somebody that treats you better and accepts you as you are? Then you believe that you deserve something better. This can be applied to all other things: to your job, life itself, family, education, friends. Or as Henry Ford once used to say, "Whether you think you can or you think you can't, you're always right." Inside and out.

What it was about my former partner, and I do not like to admit it, was exactly the same. I thought I had to earn love. It was not about him at all. It was about my attitude, my value that I felt was so low at that point in time. I was lonely, sad, had self-doubts, and hardly any direction and goals. And there he was, my counterpart, with the exact same feelings, only worse. I spent years trying to make him realize how loveable he was and that he did not need to hide, did not have to earn anything, because, despite all his weaknesses, he was fine the way he was and I loved him as he was. It was not until two years later that I understood that **I** had to learn it rather than teach it to him.

In addition, it was at the time that I learned essential lessons in the sense of abilities. My partner at the time was the exaggerated version of what I could not yet do: self-love, confidence, open and honest communication, assertiveness, consistency, and much more.

Tip 12: Take your shadow and go

Very often, whenever we are rejected, we find ourselves again in the nagging victim position and think or say sentences such as, "How could you hurt me so?", "Why did you do that?", "I would have never... I never would... I have never...", "For years I have done this and that and this is how you thank me?", "I loved you and you?" The same thing also happens to us in other life situations. When we lose our job, have misunderstandings with friends, or only fight with our partner. We do not want to be guilty and, therefore, pass on any duty and responsibility to unburden ourselves. But more than anything, we do not want to raise the thoughts that we are "wrong". This behavior is unfortunately double-edged. On the one hand, we transfer all the responsibility to someone else and turn away from our self-responsibility and participation. We pin it on a second person who is then in a tight spot in case they cannot expressly free themselves and say no. In this way, it cannot lead to genuine compromises. In contrast, you built fronts.

On the other hand, were the accusations, rebukes, emotional blackmail that trigger guilt and self-doubt in others supposed to make the other person think about things differently, take you more seriously, and love you? There is one thing that I have learned, as torturous and difficult as it was, whenever you "win" somebody, it may happen that you have to fight again every single time, every morning, every evening, for so long, until you lose one morning on the way to work, while you let your guard down. Without realizing.

When we feel lonely or are afraid of being alone, we act similarly. Either we say that it is the other person's fault and responsibility and we pass a weight onto them that they cannot carry on their own. Or we excuse their irresponsibility and take over all of it. In my opinion, it is difficult to go both ways.

When loneliness or times alone become so constricting that it takes your breath away, remind yourself of your self-responsibility. Everything that is supposed to be permanent must be a balance of giving and taking. Everything else would be too painful in the long term.

Tip 13: Autogenic training

As a seminar leader of this relaxation technique and expert in the field of anxiety, I have studied various relaxation methods for their effects on anxiety. Autogenic training offers you an effective and individual method of relaxation tailored to your needs at that moment.

It is a form of physical relaxation that relaxes the entire body through repetitions (muscle relaxation). In autogenic training, weight, warmth, breathing regulation, heart regulation, abdominal warmth, and forehead cooling are generated *automatically* for a relaxation that comes from within. This, in turn, calms the mind and stills stress, worries, and fears. Autogenic training can very easily be used anywhere by anyone alone, once learned and practiced sufficiently. The groundwork forms the suggestion of a state of peace in the individual regions of the body. Through the repetitions, our brain automatically learns to retrieve this peace. In their effectiveness, autosuggestions can be remembered extremely easily – in all situations.

Autogenic training is based on a scientifically proven learning technique of the brain: suggestion. Suggestion stimulates the brain to create new neuronal connections that cause relaxation automatically, on demand, and restore calmness and peace. Anyone can apply this relaxation technique without prior knowledge. Autogenic training is therefore not a miracle but a suggestion of calmness achieved through training. This also means that it should be repeated multiple times to achieve the full effect. Autogenic training can help against:

- Anxiety and panic
- Allergies
- Asthma
- Problems with blood pressure
- Eating disorders
- Skin diseases
- Arrhythmia
- Headaches and migraines
- Neurodermitis
- Psychosomatic problems
- All kinds of pain
- Mental disorders
- Sexual dysfunction
- Addictions
- and much more.

In autogenic training (AT for short), you talk about a basic level (for beginners) and advanced level (for advanced users). The basic level contains similar phrases everywhere, but there are differences in the phrases for the abdomen and/or term for a heartbeat. My autogenic training contains these phrases:

I am completely calm and relaxed.
My right arm is very heavy.
My left arm is very heavy.
My right leg is very heavy.
My left leg is very heavy.
My arms and legs are very heavy, comfortably heavy.
My right arm is comfortably warm.
My left arm is comfortably warm.
My right leg is comfortably warm.
My left leg is comfortably warm.
My arms and legs are very warm, comfortably warm.
My breathing is calm and even.
My pulse is calm and even.
My solar plexus is comfortably warm.
My head is free and clear.
My forehead is comfortably cool.

In the specialized training programs for advanced users, further helpful suggestions follow these phrases.

Instructions: How an autogenic training session works

Go on YouTube or visit a store you trust and choose an autogenic training program. It should be between 15 and 30 minutes in order to achieve an optimum effect on beginners. Make yourself comfortable, lie or sit down in a quiet place where you can relax undisturbed, without being interrupted by noise. It is recommended that you use headphones in order to deepen the relaxation. Start the respective training.

The training programs should, if possible, be listened to several times a week in order to obtain the effect of autosuggestion more quickly and sustainably. The optimum dose would be once a day, whether on the train to work or when going to sleep. Try to relax with autogenic training at least 1-2 times a week.

Autogenic training with and without recirculation

Training sessions with recirculation can be carried out throughout the day. At the end of the training session, you are guided from 1 to 10 back into the awake and clear state. These training programs are not meant for falling asleep.

Training sessions without recirculation should only be carried out when you can/want to fall asleep while listening. They are ideal for use in the evening in bed as a sleeping aid. They end automatically; the background music slowly fades out.

Tip 14: Take the worst and make the best of it

Have you ever asked yourself what message for your life is hidden behind the fear or loneliness? I mean "message" in the sense of "subject". Which subject is hidden within you, what led you to walk your current path, or what won't let you leave it? And above all, what can this path still bring you?

Find the subject and think about how you would like to resolve it. Put yourself in the center and view yourself as an outsider. Think of your contours and limits and then make the best of them.

This approach is behaviorally therapeutic, the form of therapy that most people find to be the most difficult. They have to learn to break up their inner resistance by themselves. I, too, had to draw lessons from my fear and loneliness that, although painful, were necessary and helpful.

INCONVENIENT TRUTHS

What Loneliness and the Fear of Being Alone Taught Me

"Pray that your loneliness may spur you into finding something to live for, great enough to die for."

- Dag Hammarskjold

Everybody experiences fear as cruel, inconvenient, and obstructive. Until today, I have had to learn that fear has a benevolent side to it that I never want to do without ever again. Every time that I have anxiety, it forces me to ask myself, "What do you want?", "What do I have to know?", "What do I have to do to make you milder?" And every time, I receive valuable answers that pave the way for my next steps – towards more self-realization, self-actualization, well-being, and balance.

As part of this book, I would like to share some of my realizations from my fear and panic times with you, even if your fear does not necessarily coincide with mine (especially in combination with panic attacks). Perhaps you may just find new impulses for your life in my lessons.

1. Everything has its limits. Fear shows you yours.

I was always good at dealing with unfamiliar boundaries. I took them into account, I perceived them without people having to remind me of them. I never needed harsh words to let others have time or needs. By contrast, I took most people to be more important than me too often. In my head, I wanted these people to do well. I wanted to contribute to it. But I was inwardly hoping that I would get something back for it. I was often disappointed in this assumption, even by the people from whom I had least expected it.

In doing so, I realized I have limits (too). The "truth" of the past was however that I seriously believed I had none. I thought I could give and carry and afford and endure infinitely. Although I was aware of my needs, I rarely maintained them in discussions, did not stick with them long enough, or demanded much too little when I believed that somebody else needed more than I did.

My external orientation regularly ran into my internal one. It really hurt me whenever people only expected and demanded and waited for their desired result. As if it was obvious.

Naturally, this was largely down to me. People were used to me stepping back and letting them go ahead, being responsible for them, fighting together with them, caring for, looking after, and acting for them. In those days, I was often conflicted that I had to make decisions – between my own and foreign limits. This also means that I had to choose between my anguish and the potential suffering of others. Unfortunately, I often decided for my own pain instead of returning self-responsibility to people. It caused me to lose my footing. At some point, there was no longer any room where I was important or where I could provide for myself in the first place. There were only the others and what I could/should/had to do for them in order to *possibly* be liked.

Sensing no more footing pushed me into my agoraphobia. Everything fell down on me, like this typical agoraphobia feeling that the whole sky is crashing down on you and weighing you down. You can't hold on to anything and can't orientate yourself around anything or anyone. Agoraphobia is the symptom that you have lost your footing (in you and on you) and, externally, that you no longer have anything tangible in your hands. You grasp into the emptiness that threatens to crush you, similar to depression.

2. Nothing is self-evident. But fear shows you that you have to make yourself evident.

I was a true master at causing as few problems for those I cared about as possible. I basically endured pain for at least four years longer than other people. As already mentioned, I was tough.

I, therefore, kept most of my problems and troubles hidden from others. I don't want to say that I always lied or did what was best. I concentrated only on my opposite so that all the attention – and unfortunately, there was a lot who did not notice it at all – then fell on the others. Very few asked how I was doing, what I was doing, how I was coping, what had become of one thing, or how the other had been resolved. No inquiries, usually only satisfaction that they were in the center, while they had the feeling that everything was fine with me. For a long time, this worked very well. I did not have to discuss my issues and could also minimize those before me. I did not burden anyone or give them concerns that distracted them from their own.

I know now that that was a mistake. I would have been able to and have had to open myself to a lot of people. I would have even had to ask some people to hold back in line with mutuality, completely regardless of what they were carrying around in life. I would have had to separate myself, if necessary, from my (wrong) consideration, my (apparent) toughness, and definitely from a few people in order to get closer to myself. But keeping everything within was wrong.

Human beings need other human beings. Everybody needs help sometimes as well as a strong shoulder that will not pull away and which says, "You're going to be okay!"

3. Panic is panic about and because of yourself.

Especially my panic attacks, which went hand in hand with the agoraphobia, were due to this fault in myself and my environment. I had suppressed so much (of my own needs, values, goals, and feelings), kept secrets from myself, and not revealed to others that a giant mountain of anger, fear, and sorrow had formed into a negative ball of energy that offloaded into the most impossible situations.

For example, with waiting processes, I did not want more, to line up for others, or to wait in my own life. I no longer had any patience for anything in the world. I had waited long enough, persevered for so long, and shown consideration, played ping pong with my soul, and led it to believe, "Soon, Little One, soon it will be your turn too!" I could not wait one second longer for MYSELF and my satisfaction. I wanted it NOW. Straight away, then and there, and it did not matter at all who it hurt. The rope was torn. And it was my own mistake, because I had put strain on it long enough by letting myself and my goals out of my sight.

Or we take the long route. With panic, we can only cover distance with difficulty, whether it lasts two minutes or ten. Being completely silent on long bus and train rides. I usually suffered from this because I had no more strength to go long journeys for others, only half-heartedly, without ever (spiritually and emotionally) arriving. I had walked so many paths for others because I wrongly believed that I would also find myself in their goal, that suddenly, I was unable to have even five minutes to myself on the way. For me, this worked in the real and figurative sense. My previous long-distance relationship had completely worn me out. My spiritual running around the fulfillment of unfamiliar goals had burned me out emotionally.

It was as if my fear had said, "You did not move for yourself earlier either! Previously, there were only foreign goals too! Now look closely at what you are doing with yourself! Either you learn to look and decide whether the goal is also for you, whether the path is perhaps to rocky for you, if you want to go in a completely different direction, or you remain motionless through me until you have understood it. It is either your goal (also great, common goals) or it is a foreign goal. Whether you pursue it or not, the choice is up to you."

My fear was right. Nobody, no job, no task, no dirty dishes, no unnecessary request or "problem" of a friend should ever be so important that you forget yourself or your needs.

And then there's still this point – people who I had little interest in but with whom I still spent my time. I no longer know why and what for. But I spent a lot of time with false niceness towards people for whom I was fully replaceable, who would no longer be able to remember me the next day, make me wait, or leave me standing.

I was partly also this way myself. I looked for a lot of sympathy in people who I did not find very sympathetic so that I would be able to love them. Therefore, I spent time hanging out with supposedly interesting people who bored me in reality. I had to admit to myself that you cannot get on well with everybody and that you simply do not share a lot of values with some. You will always have different opinions or rub someone the wrong way and vice versa.

The moments where I acted as if everything was tutti-frutti, and my opposite was more important than me, were always bordered with panic attacks. Because I could not have been more inauthentic. My panic spoke to me. "Be authentic and make yourself at long last content, by going your own way to your own goals, even with separations if need be."

4. Recognition is a traitor.

When I am writing this, I am in my mid-30s and, if I am completely honest, I have to admit that for around 33 of my 34 years, I had to fight for respect in one or the other area. Usually for little to nothing too. I asked myself internally whether I was prepared to fight another 33 years for external recognition. I answered in my head with, "Hm. Perhaps yes. If I would get it then too."

I promised myself that I would hold out for each of the next 33 years. Again. The hope of finding what I so strongly hoped for and desired within this time made me happy. With all the rejection and disappointment included – because that was the risk that I would have to take again. Then I asked myself, "You would therefore really fight another 33 years for recognition, day in, day out, impose such a long and hard struggle on yourself, just to be recognized a few times in the meantime? But you are not ready to give yourself this recognition each day and to save yourself from being disappointed by others?"

And I myself am probably overlooking one or the other area of life right now, where I want recognition *mixed up with love, acceptance, and belonging,* although I am and have my own strength.

External recognition will always betray you if you are not ready to value and recognize yourself.

5. Comparing with others only leads back to you.

Those who look eagerly will find jealousy.
Those who believe they are not good enough will find someone who treats them as such.

There will always be someone who is better. Always. This is something that I have learned. There will always be fears of losing your partner, or your money, or your job, or the support of a friend.

However, there is this state where you can make yourself aware that you are fine as you are, and can and always should learn it. Those who have a different opinion, have an opinion that they still do not have to share for this reason.

Whenever someone judges you badly, that says more about them than you. Those who don't like you are looking for somebody else. That says something about them but nothing about you and your worth. Your worth will always remain.

6. Many people do not need closeness. They need distance.

Closeness and distance are important aspects of fear and sorrow. It is also important to know that feeling both feelings often gets mixed up and exaggerated, replaced, or confused.

As such, many of those affected confuse closeness with themselves with closeness to others. They would avoid distance in order to avoid closeness with themselves, which also means that they would have to endure emptiness but not yet dare to. And there are those who rather fear closeness to others because then they could lose closeness with themselves.

Thirdly, there are people who, in truth, don't want *not too much closeness* but rather need more freedom for themselves. They tend to view it in an exaggerated way, because the fear in the form of people and the fear of potential conflict situations messes things up for them. Then it appears as if they could no longer put up with, listen to, spend time with, share a room with anyone.

I still know how often I wanted to have the whole world just for me. Once, on the morning train to a conference, I was so ecstatic about the five! people in the whole carriage that I spent the most relaxing time of my life on the train. This is the need of the soul/the spirit for fewer distractions, less noise, less overstimulation, more me-time, more peace, more contact, instead of rush, pressure, to-do lists, chatty people, and squeaky wheels.

Whenever you want peace, retreat, and distance, it is usually others who quickly say to you, "You are so distant." This happened to me immediately at the start. Although I previously had had no daily contact with my friends, back then it was felt as if they had never wanted more contact with me. Not to stand by me, but rather because they saw my withdrawal as a separation from them.

However, many people don't quite need closeness to other people but rather distance in order to recreate closeness with themselves and to sense it again. In my opinion, that is completely okay, even if it needs a demand for explanation in their environment. But everyone can and is allowed to decide for themselves what they can do and want to give. Sometimes you also need an occasional "withdrawn, everything, opaque, stubborn, cold, selfish" behavior. These are naturally the attributes that society would use. Because I myself was often confronted with these attributes, I find *when I am doing well, then it does me good. So, I do it.* And I know, just the same, times will come again where it will be the opposite.

Sometimes you only need closeness with yourself or want to completely savor the regained closeness and determine your position: Where do I stand? Where do I still want to go in life? What do I want to see realized in my life at all costs? What can I do to support myself in this? What do I do that objects this and rather hinders me?

Fear of being alone and of loneliness can also be a signal that you don't want to ask yourself these questions. Many people do want to learn more about themselves but are then too afraid of the next steps. It is what is known as a "Schwellenangst", describing the fear you feel before you take an important step in life. Check whether you only fear the next steps because you have to cross a threshold, behind which could be a completely new life. If you become aware of this threshold, the frightening feelings will gradually become resolved. We often only have to allow our unpleasant feelings in changes, because suppressing them would only make them more powerful.

Those who deep down long for a refuge from the noise of the world, who are introverted or highly sensitive, highly gifted, or very empathetic, should not hide from their needs or work against them. Allow them to be and accept that your needs have consequences that can feel good for you.

7. I need less things to be happy than I thought.

In a situation of mental strain, you quickly notice everything that you *don't* need. Material things suddenly become meaningless. People who had previously seemed so important suddenly disappear from our thoughts, only popping up here and there. The rest seems unimportant because you have to deal with yourself and your situation. As they say, you can't make an omelet without breaking any eggs.

In 2013, I realized that I only need these 10 things in life to feel satisfied:

1. Nature and animals
2. Peace and quiet
3. Physical strength that I only notice when jogging, lifting weights, or doing kick yoga
4. A bicycle
5. Fresh air and daylight
6. A healthy diet
7. A lot of sleep
8. A pen and paper for writing
9. One understanding and supportive person, instead of thoughtless, critical people
10. A stubborn person who reminds me of my stubbornness

I do not miss any of what we are led to believe we need to be happy in the world. At that time, I didn't miss my house, farm, car, fancy holidays, or piles of money, nor did I miss the security of my family or parties. To me, that is the dearest lesson of all, because I know that I can be entirely content and happy every day with so little.

What would you call a must in your life? On the next page, you can create your own overview of happiness.

Happiness list

Make a list of everything that you need to feel emotionally secure. Consciously consider the areas that you have already achieved. Try to name at least 10 aspects. Only then turn to the aspects that you believe you still lack.

8. There will always be people who do not understand you.

It is highly likely that these include some of the closest people in your life. A fish doesn't even know that it is swimming in water. It has never known any other life. Wanting to explain that to it is a difficult task.

It is the same way with fear and sadness. People who have never felt it are unable to have any emotional understanding of what it is like to live with it. Nor are they ever in the position to give you constructive advice about it. This requires a good deal of empathy in order to truly empathize. Not everyone is capable of this. Even the best therapists can fail at this because their theory books from actual practice differ significantly.

Back then, I really suffered from this, because there were friends and family members who did not understand it. Some of them still asked again and again about the same things, although I had explained several times that I could not do it. "Just do this and that and don't be like that! *Just* do it already!"

Some were surprised that I could no longer be there for them, could no longer put them in the center like usual, no longer immediately scream YES! to everything that they suggested. Others asked me how I was faring, how I felt, watched me down to the last detail, summed up their impressions, and settled in. There are exactly two ways and both are understandable and okay.

9. What is not to be is not to be.

I was not somebody who hung on to avoidance, but there were moments in which I noticed something. Behind the situations where others spoke of avoidance behavior, there were situations hidden within me that I generally had no interest in (anymore).

Here, the point of mutuality that was meant to/wanted to set in was crucial. After some time, I knew very quickly when I was only afraid of the fear and when I really had no interest in the situation, the person, or the goal.

Admitting this to myself (and others) was indeed often futile and difficult, but it was necessary.

EPILOG

You Often Find the Greatest Lesson Through Emptiness

Fall in love with your courage.
Become so strong that your soul attracts what is intended for it.

- Proverbs

Admitting at all that sadness, loneliness, fear, and anger also comes with a thorough portion of positives is not easy. But for me, it was the first step towards more self-responsibility, capacity for action, and a convergence on the great topic of becoming an adult. That means nevertheless coping with whatever comes your way in adult life. In this way, I learned that everything good also has bad parts that you are responsible for, have to comply with, and that every goal brings a path with it, that every relationship also has its downs, and that dealing with what you have is what shows you your true size. What matters is how you react to the emptiness and downs, not that they are there. Because there will always be bad times.

My fear and panic showed me that not everybody was meant to be in my life, I did not have to be nice to everybody, cannot be the center for everyone, or need to crawl around in the background. It showed me my value, the little I had to do with it, the little that I awarded myself, the amount that I wanted, and the little that I pursued, allowed myself, and took out.

In my eyes, feelings are an excellent way of confronting yourself with the individual rough edges of your personality. Through my fear, I was able to learn that I will never be perfect and that it is completely unnecessary to impress anyone else. What I do for myself, I do for me. What I do against myself, I direct against me. Both are part of my life decision, and I can correct them each individual day if I want to. But I cannot give anyone the "blame" for my life. I am responsible for everything I do and refrain from.

Nor was it ever the fault of my feelings. In contrast, they were my shield of protection against everything that I believed to be worth nothing, to not be able to do, to not be allowed to do, and to not be supposed to do. In doing so, only I was always responsible for my feelings. Just like you are responsible for yours. I feared that I had only partially fulfilled this responsibility for many years. How is it with you?

Today, I believe that the only reason for my anxiety disorder was finally waking up.

THE EMERGENCY IDEA CHEST

A Distraction Please! 54 Impulses for Activities

These are my top ideas for when the fear of being alone again intrudes or you find yourself again in the middle of an atmosphere of emptiness, displeasure, and lethargy. Some of them require other people, but the majority can easily be carried out alone.

All these ideas should help you to pull yourself out of your victimization and to take your life into your own hands. They should pull you away from helplessness and conjure up a bit of energy. But please bear in mind, you are the magician. You hold the magic wand in your hand. Wave it when the time is right. Or simply open this book whenever the threatening feelings grasp you again. Do something different from this list every day and begin from the start again whenever you have tried out each idea once. In this way, you can reactivate the list of your passions and take action for yourself. And who knows? Perhaps you will even discover something new.

When you find that an idea is fun for you and/or helps you, put a checkmark or a smiley next to it. Later, anytime you are bored again or sad, you can go back to the list and remind yourself of it.

1. What is for dinner tonight? How about an exotic, unfamiliar dish? Find a recipe website online and choose a type of cuisine that you do not know or have not enjoyed for a long time. Write down the necessary ingredients. Take your feelings and go shopping. Whenever you are back home again, enjoy your time cooking, for example, with good music.

2. Write to three people and ask them for a film recommendation. Look for the films on the internet or go to a video store. Enjoy the films and delight in their stories.

3. Think about or look for a place from where you can watch children and/or animals. The cuteness will stimulate the production of your happy hormones. Additionally, you will be out in the fresh air, stimulating your vitamin D levels from the daylight, which will strengthen you both mentally and physically. However, do not compare anything, just enjoy the happiness of the children/animals and take part in their energy for life.

4. Name three songs that you used to enjoy listening to as a teenager. If you don't have access to them on analog/digital channels, then go on video and music portals and listen to them. If it has a fast beat, dance to it. Sing along. Think back on the good memories from that time.

5. Send the following message to three to five (or more) people that know you well: *"Don't ask: I am sitting in a seminar right now. Can you please name three qualities that make me special in the next 60 minutes? Thanks!"* I myself learned this game in a seminar. The results that people sent back to me were astounding and – very uplifting. Ever since then I have really known my strengths and, above all, I appreciate them far more than ever. It also gave me the feeling that not only did my worth exist, but it was also greater than I had previously thought.

6. Photography is a wonderful hobby that I would recommend to anyone who does not really know what to do with themselves. Firstly, it costs as good as nothing, as most people have a smartphone these days that can take photos. Those who, however, want to become a bit of an expert can still add the appropriate equipment. Photography allows you the chance to be outside and among people while having something to do. Photography is a creative task and stimulates the right side of the brain. At the same time, you busy yourself with motifs that you find

interesting. In doing so, photography creates meaning and activity, awakens inspiration and creativity, and, with it, promotes healing on all levels.

7. Try following another's footsteps. I invented this technique when I was looking for ways to remove myself from worries, fears, and painful realities. I thought that I would get a clearer view to be able to make decisions. Above all, I wanted to step away from my thoughts, which, at the time, had negative effects on my actions and left me unable to act at all. My worries at the time provoked stiffness within me. Thanks to this technique, I found a way out, which is why I am passing it on to you. "Following Another's Footsteps" is like a foreign biography work. You choose a person that you admire and are so interested in that you want to find out everything about them and their life, work, and thoughts. It could be big celebrities from history or lesser-known people. Depending on the choice, you will make an appropriately quick and broad find.

8. You can also do a biography work within your own family. Genealogy research is easier than ever today. Thanks to extensive online directories, you can pick up on clues and achieve quick results. In genealogy databases, you can find digitalized timelines, address books, censuses, birth, marriage, and death registrations, immigration and emigration information,

electoral registers, military lists, church books, passenger manifests, and other documents from long forgotten times. Genealogy research creates closeness and familiarity. It is something that you can deeply delve into that can nurture you and restore you. So, which person from your family would you like to find out more about?

9. Go on another's journey. A variation of the footsteps hunt is choosing a role. Who inspires you? Who do you admire for something? Find out how the person did, achieved, and changed something and imitate their ways. Take a walk in their shoes and move around in them. Those who have trouble animating and motivating themselves to something can profit from the strength of others. The ignorance is often about possible and necessary steps that prevent us from making beneficial changes.

10. Inspiring films can wipe away any pain. As a qualified media scholar, I adore films for their characteristic of awakening hope and inspiration for new paths and perspectives. The film industry has produced whole truckloads of films for people who are going through transition phases or standstills in their life.

11. Everybody needs an anthem. Those who are familiar with the series "Ally McBeal" are sure to remember that Ally and her colleague John had one. They chose

a song as an anthem that they would immediately and emotionally pull out from all stressful and frightening situations. The stimulating anthems then transform the negative feelings into courage, joy, and confidence. You can listen to the anthem or, even better, let it play in your head like music. It will be a catchy tune for more strength, self-empowerment, and satisfaction!

12. Remember a stressful moment in which you were happy that you would soon be alone again. Perhaps it was a stressful day at work or you felt trapped and/or overwhelmed due to other circumstances and simply wanted to go home, out of a group, away from other people – and be alone. Simply the memory of this can retrieve feelings again, which your brain will reflect. Remembering such moments calms you down whenever you are gripped by anxiety.[13]

13. Try the Hand on heart method. You rub your heart and the surrounding region of the body with essential oils and creams. The spreads warmth and is also calming due to your own touch. Alternatively, you can place your hands on your heart and let them rest there while you close your eyes and breathe. I have even sometimes done this on the train and anywhere else. And no one found it strange either.

---

[13] cf. Winch 2013

14. Give yourself a hug. This closeness exercise is so simple yet effective that it only requires a few words. You join your elbow with your chest and lay only your hands on your shoulder blades. In difficult moments, you can hug and be there for yourself. I had a few clients who found this form of support very helpful. The exercise nurtured acceptance and tolerance of their own feelings and spread comfort. Science has proven that a touch, even lasting seconds, strengthens well-being and the immune system in general. No other people are necessary. We can do this ourselves.

15. Go online and look for the song "Weightless" by Marconi Union on YouTube, Vimeo, or Spotify. It was made specially to reduce stress. British studies have found out that it reduces a person's stress by 65%. For this reason, it is recommended that you do not listen to it while driving.[14]

16. When was the last time that you drew and painted? When I was in the middle of my panic disorder, I began to draw again. At some point, I painted in all situations, right to the airplane. It calmed my fear, guided my attention to something else, lifted me out of my broodings, and allowed me to concentrate on myself. Not only can you learn to paint, but you don't have to be good at it either. There are piles of offers in stores such as coloring books, zentangles, and

---

[14] cf. Curtin 2016

paint-by-numbers. Last but not least, you can find classes at your local adult education center from sketching, nude painting, and watercolor painting to comic and children's book illustration.

17. When was the last time that you wrote somebody a letter? Everything runs digitally today. We are used to quickly and inattentively hitting the keys and establishing communication straight away. Yet letters are still one of the most personal and beneficial forms of contact.

18. Writing is considered by conventional medicine to have a healing effect. Those who can enjoy that have an endless number of possibilities open to them: poems, haikus, short stories, novels, experimental texts, blogs, reviews. The various genres further the opportunities even further. Writing courses or free online offers can quickly and effectively help to get the ball rolling.

19. Which people that you have not seen in a long time do you remember fondly? If you still have their contact details, get in touch with them again. If you no longer have any contact details for them, find the person online or through mutual friends and acquaintances! This can become an exciting journey into your past.

20. What have you always wanted to do? Travel around the world, plant a tree, go on a cruise? Whatever you dream of, buy a book or visit a website that deals with the subject. Let yourself be whisked away to a different world. Immerse yourself in your dream and form strength using your imagination! Imagination techniques work true wonders.

21. What hobby have you always wanted to learn? Here, too, buy a book on the subject and read everything that you have to know. See whether you can practice this hobby in your area. See if there are like-minded people in your area or suggest the subject in clubs, the adult education center, or other institutions. Perhaps you are not the only one who is interested in it.

22. Video games help against anxiety. The internet has dozens of options for playing in a so-called community or in teams. In this way, you are not playing alone and, at the same time, you have an activity that stimulates your spirit as well as reduces any fears and worries you may have.

23. Keep a success journal. Whatever goal you have planned, a success journal can help you. It is recommended that you note down your small successes or great breakthroughs every day. It makes you happy, gives you more confidence, and, above all, hope - to set aside negative feelings.

24. Keep a gratitude journal. This kind of journal is enhancing. You can note down what you are grateful for every day. What made you particularly happy today? Or what are you thankful for, even if your life may be somewhat more difficult at the moment? If a day has not been so good, think of all the other circumstances in your life that you are grateful for, and there are certainly a few. We are often very biased when we have something negative in our life and completely forget the good things that are there.

25. Be creative. Use the right half of your brain more than your left. Leave the thoughts and come to the creativity. I would like to give you some examples that can have an art therapeutic effect throughout the creative process. Create a poster with your feelings or fears. Print them out in photos and newspaper and magazine cut-outs. Give them headings and expand them with quotes. Another similar example is the so-called vision board. On this poster, stick and write everything you still have planned for your life: trips, endeavors, activities, hobbies. Another form of this kind of board is what I call the "Because I love myself". On this, stick and write everything that you love about yourself. Yes, there are wonderful and unique qualities in you. Think about this and you will quickly determine that, while there may be many suppressed and unfulfilled needs within you, you are still a lovely person. Print exactly this fact on the board. Hang it

somewhere you can see it so that you can always be reminded of it, in case negative feelings should get out of hand.

26. If you expect to be disappointed by people, create a list of all the impossible limits. Promise yourself that you will abide by these during your next social contacts – for your sake.

27. Start the day with Morning Pages[15]. This technique comes from the author Julia Cameron. She developed it for people who have stopped or suppressed their creativity and intuition. It basically works as follows: Each morning, you write – before doing anything else – three pages full of everything that is in your head: from doing laundry, children and duties, work, unwillingness and anger, thoughts that you do not say out loud and so on. Write without setting the pen down and, in doing so, unload your brain. Through this, you enrich yourself because you take your thoughts and feelings seriously and let them be. Through writing, we make space for new thoughts and empty the trash with everything that we have to but actually do not want, should do, and want to postpone.

28. End the day with Evening Pages. An Evening Pages exercise has been developed from Morning Pages.

---
[15] cf. Cameron 2009

Since the Morning Pages technique gains such wonderful results, stressed or anxious people should also use it before they go to sleep at night. In this way, nothing is rolling around in your head whenever you want to/have to go to sleep. Everything is back where it belongs, and your brain is relieved from the baggage of the day. It will not be any less. In this way, you can reflect, meditate through writing, and lighten yourself twice a day.

29. Meditate. For everyone who doesn't think they can begin meditating – my explanation is different. I experience meditation as permission to sit down and steer your thoughts to NOTHING. This requires a certain amount of practice, but the effects are enormous. Those who have sorrow, fear, and panic, therefore only have to deal with occupying their thoughts with nothing. Empty the mind, as they say. It is easier said than done. I know that from experience. However, I believe 10 minutes each day are sufficient. It is a necessary exercise for recognizing that you yourself can become a danger to yourself when you see dangers or emptiness everywhere or do not appreciate yourself and/or others enough. *You are safe!* is a realization that meditations want to give to you. Let yourself relax and tap into your core, which will support you here. Meditation also has the right answer for the big question "What should I do?" Inspirations that come from you during

meditation are more valuable than any counselor. As an aside, I prefer Deepak Chopra's meditations. He also has an app and, above all, offers free meditations on different subjects at regular intervals. Simply look in the App Store and try it out. His meditations are produced specially to allow beginners to be well looked after.

30. Read your favorite book. Also, take a look at whether the author has written any new books.

31. Research online whether forums exist that deal with this piece of literature and exchange views on it. This could be a wonderful opportunity to establish new contacts.

32. There are subjects of all kinds, relevant forums, and group meetings (not just online) for all interests. If you spend some time researching these, you are sure to find nice, like-minded people.

33. Listen to your favorite song or a song from your past that reminds you of nice, happy times. For me, songs from my youth worked very well, where I felt free and self-determined.

34. Take random photos of the surrounding area with your smartphone. Concentrate on beautiful motifs that are ideally a bit further away from you. The

feeling of expanse through a small pattern on your phone screen is less scary and releases your thoughts from the negative loop.

35. If there are no animals near you, then YouTube or Facebook videos of animals can help. When many people were amazed at the cat video hype, there was a good reason why it worked and went viral – they make people happy. They are cute. They direct your attention to something fragile and needy. They activate your protection and caring mechanisms. Ergo, happiness hormones are secreted and stress hormones fall. At the same time, your psyche is properly unburdened and bad thoughts disappear almost on their own.

36. You can also apply the 60-second smile method without children or animals. Simply raise the corners of your mouth and smile, even if you don't feel like it. Through this, you will send the opposite signal to your brain. It has to allow the stress hormones to leave and, instead, secrete positive ones.

37. Hum a positive melody or a song that spontaneously comes to mind during your anxiety or sorrow.

38. Carry a talisman that you can hold on to whenever you feel prone to getting an anxiety attack.

39. Write a poem about what the fear and sadness are doing in you at the moment. Writing therapy has – as studies have shown since the 1980s – a significantly positive effect on the emotional state, on both depression and fears. For this reason, writing therapy is often used in "traditional", state-recognized therapy, whether in a clinic or one to one with a psychologist.

40. Consciously breathe air into your head or into the place in your body where you most feel anxiety or panic. With every breath, imagine the air that you have breathed in flowing through and purifying it.

41. Stretch your body. Create width in your chest by opening your arms and stretching them wide, spreading your feet shoulder-width apart, and taking up the room with your posture. Amy Cuddy[16] from Harvard University researched stress levels in various wide or tight body postures. She discovered that a lot of stress hormones were secreted with tight postures and a lot of testosterone with wide, manly postures. And the brain again joins in.

42. Sing. Using your own voice is one of the best mental hygiene tricks there is. What's more, the trick is not at all new, just rarely discussed. Singing keeps you mentally healthy.

---

[16] cf. Cuddy 2012

43. Dance too. As such, the Australian company NLNL (No Lights No Lycra) started a worldwide offensive to encourage people both in company and alone to indulge in a dance to a random song as a break once a day. They also have an app (No Light No Lycra by NLNL), as the events have not yet arrived everywhere in the world.

44. What was the #1 song in the charts on the day you were born? You can find your song on a number of websites. Find it, dance to it, and/or listen to the song whenever you are feeling anxious again. It will remind you that your life is worth too much to be anxious.

45. Saying affirmations, such as *"I am without fear"* or *"Being alone is meaningless"*, can also help. Although they do not properly penetrate your long-term memory until after 30 to 60 days of practice, if you keep up, you can be saved a few painful broodings. Affirmations are broader than mantras.

46. Similar to affirmations, mantras can generate positive thoughts or distract from negative ones in the short term. Mantras are rather sound-emitting bodies that can be sung as well as spoken. Thus, you use them in meditations or chant (sing) them – if you really want to do in the "proper" Buddhist way with the famous Om. However, you have to believe in the profound meaning (and know it). A popular mantra for every

day is, *"Everything in life comes to me with lightness and joy and splendor!"* You can find a variation of this in my mp3 autogenic training programs where I use similar mantras. But they are spoken so slowly that the meaning is easy to grasp – *I. Am. Completely. Relaxed.* Every single word of a mantra counts.

47. As already mentioned, cooking is an excellent method for people who have a pure desire for food and, at the same time, feel alone. Many entrepreneurs are aware of this and have made a business out of this with loneliness. In the meantime, several activities are offered that combine cooking with getting to know new people. You book a place online and, after selecting a time and successful payment, you receive the location and other details. Then the meeting takes place, usually in the apartment of the new person or in your own. Two people, who previously did not know each other, then prepare the menu for, often, four other new people who join later. You all sit together at the table, eat, and get to know each other. The appetizer, main course, and dessert are prepared in the homes of the other participants, depending on the offer, and you enjoy all the individual courses together. The prices vary greatly. However, such an offer could well be worth it for those who enjoy cooking. But you do not necessarily have to cook with somebody. It can also become a solo passion that provides something to hold on to. Thinking

about what there is to eat beforehand, shopping for ingredients, preparing them, and eating them. All of this is pure love and takes time. Time that you do not spend brooding or with sadness but rather with yourself. When you then cook healthy, you do something good for your body instead of feeling flabby or tired after your meal. The brain remembers moments like these. Instead of reaching for the pizza menu or running to your favorite kebab stall next time you feel lonely, you could cook your favorite meal.

48. Gardening is one of the best methods, which is why it is located far up the list of the best stress management techniques. Why? You participate in growth, see it grow, nurture and care for it, look after it in wind and other types of weather, and supply it with water to nourish it when it is too hot. At the end, you have raised a plant. You yourself have sown life. In the same way, the smell of the earth, working with and in the earth is calming and stimulates your inner peace. It grounds you in the truest sense of the word.

49. Clean. Yes, seriously. The reason why this trick works so well is that cleaning gets you moving physically and, at the end, you are left with a clean product that you have made. You can see that you were the one who tidied up your apartment or house. If you can keep your living areas clean, then you can also have

some order in your life. On the outside, and likewise on the inside.

50. Cleaning windows is a similar tip that brings transparency and clarity (on a whole new metaphorical level). Cleaning windows (if you do it properly with cloths and polishing cloths) is also a strenuous activity where you can vent your aggressions. Even taking out the trash and clearing out is considered a cleaning ritual. It is not without reason people say that minimalism makes you happy.

51. Google Maps is an excellent travel guide. When I wanted to explore the area I lived in, I took a closer look on Google Maps for places nearby: ponds, woods, lakes, parks, etc. I combined it with photography and made a hobby out of it during the spring and summer months. I was exercising in the fresh air and outdoors. It worked true wonders for my body and mind. Above all, it strengthened my self-effectiveness. Get on your bike or in your car and explore your environment.

52. Search only for "community" (in your town) as well as in surrounding towns and see what results come up. Similar search terms that you can try out to find activities and groups in your area are: club, activities, meet, meeting, group, people, getting to know.

53. Volunteer, if your time allows it. Beneficial involvements may include tutoring, supporting children with mentally ill parents, animals, older people, planning events and helping with organization, etc. If you type "volunteering (in your town)" into Google, you are sure to get a list of hits that you can check out for yourself. Helping is an activity that fulfills your heart if it does not exceed your boundaries. Furthermore, you meet like-minded people with whom you can establish wonderful acquaintances or friendships.

54. If you live in an isolated area (small town, rural area, tourist towns) or are clueless about what you can do in your area, ask your neighbor or random people that you get to know or often see at the bakery, doctor's office, in the supermarket, etc. People who have already lived somewhere for a while usually know a lot about what there is to do and where there are activities or opportunities. If everything else still fails, what would you like to do in your area? What would you like to take part in? Ask if anyone would like to get involved and put it into practice. Create the opportunities you miss yourself and/or get help to do so.

BIBLIOGRAPHY

Cameron, J. (2016). *The Artist's way: 25th Anniversary Edition. A Spiritual Path to Higher Creativity.* TarcherPerigee.

Caraso, Alain. (n/a). „Tai Chi und Psyche." *Taijiquan-Schule Ortenau.* n/a. https://taijiquan-schule-ortenau.de/content/abschlussarbeit-alaincarasco.pdf

Cuddy, A. (2012). *Amy Cuddy: Your Body Language May Shape Who You Are.* TED: https://www.ted.com/talks/amy_cuddy_your_body_language_shapes_who_you_are?language=de

Curtin, M. (26 October 2016). *Neuroscience Says Listening to This Song Reduces Anxiety by Up to 65 Percent.* Inc.com: http://www.inc.com/melanie-curtin/neuroscience-says-listening-to-this-one-song-reduces-anxiety-by-up-to-65-percent.html

Finkel, E. J., Slotter, E. B., Walton, G. M., Gross, J. J., & Luchies, L. B. (26 June 2013). A Brief Intervention to Promote Conflict Reappraisal Preserves Marital Quality Over Time. *Psychological Science, Volume: 24, Issue: 8*, S. 1595-1601.

Kaiser, S. (26 June 2016). *13 Feel-Good Movies That'll Inspire You To Follow Your Dreams.* mbg mindbodygreen: http://www.mindbodygreen.com/0-25569/13-feel-good-movies-thatll-inspire-you-to-follow-your-dreams.html

Kast, V. (2013). *Vom Sinn der Angst: Wie Ängste sich festsetzen und wie sie sich verwandeln lassen.* Freiburg im Breisgau: HERDER Spektrum.

Luhmann, M., & Hawkley, L. C. (June 2016). Age Differences in Lone-liness from Late Adolescence to Oldest Old Age. *Developmental Psychology, Volume 52(6),* S. 943-959.

Meyer, H. (3. Auflage 2009). *Jeder bekommt den Partner, den er verdient - ob er will oder nicht.* München: Arkana.

Parship Studie: Paare kommunizieren täglich 102 Minuten miteinander. (5 August 2010). Parship: https://web.parship.de/presse/pressemitteilungen/2010/PMI-Komm.Special1-050810.htm

Sciencedaily.com. (June 2014). *We speak as we feel, we feel as we speak.* ScienceDaily: https://www.sciencedaily.com/releases/2014/06/140626095717.htm

Ratner, R. K., & Hamilton, R. W. (27 April 2015). Inhibited from Bowling Alone. *Oxford University Press und Journal of Consumer Research*, S. 266-283.

Rubin, G. (17 November 2009). *Lonely and Not Happy.* Psychology Today: https://www.psychologytoday.com/blog/the-happiness-project/200911/lonely-and-not-happy

Schmale-Riedel, A. (2016). *Der unbewusste Lebensplan: Das Skript in der Transaktionsanalyse. Typische Muster und therapeutische Strategien.* München: Kösel-Verlag.

Schmidt, B. (3 August 2014). *14 Inspirational Movies Everyone Should Watch.* mbg mindbodygreen: http://www.mindbodygreen.com/0-14783/14-inspirational-movies-everyone-should-watch.html

Spezzano, C. (1997). *The Enlightment Pack: Identify Your Personal Goals, Improve Your Life, Your Work, Your Relationships. Book and 48 cards.* BulfinchPr;Har/Crds edition.

Ten Have M., de Graaf R., Monshouwer K. (n/a) *Physical exercise in adults and mental health status findings from the Netherlands mental health survey and incidence study.* November 2011. https://www.ncbi.nlm.nih.gov/pubmed/21999978.

Wetzler, S. (1993). *Living with the Passive-Aggressive Man: Coping with Hidden Aggression - From the Bedroom to the Boardroom.* Touchstone.

Winch, G. (28 June 2013). *Together but Still Lonely.* Psychology Today: https://www.psychologytoday.com/blog/the-squeaky-wheel/201306/together-still-lonely

Winch, G. (21 October 2014). *10 Surprising Facts About Loneliness.* Psychology Today: https://www.psychologytoday.com/blog/the-squeaky-wheel/201410/10-surprising-facts-about-loneliness

Winnewisser, S. (2011). *Einfach die Seele frei schreiben. Wie sich therapeutisches Schreiben auf die Psyche auswirkt.* Humboldt Verlag.

ABOUT THE AUTHOR

Janett Menzel works as a counselor, specialist journalist, and author in Berlin, Germany.

After her studies of American culture and literature, she focused on education and coaching techniques primarily for businesses. Due to her own experiences with general anxieties, panic attacks and agoraphobia, she started offering private coaching in which she spread her knowledge about underlying principles of anxieties.

At the same time, she started her very famous German blog ich-habe-auch-angst.de and quickly became one of the most influential German writers on fear and anxiety, female panic attacks, the inner child, limiting beliefs and how women can raise their self-worth. She explored stress management techniques, studied autogenous training and started a label – *trainyourmind* – with exclusive audio autogenous trainings against anxieties and panic attacks.

She is also a writer of books for kids and youngsters who happen to battle with their fear.